The **COACH** Model
FOR CHRISTIAN LEADERS

Praise for
The COACH Model for Christian Leaders

I love that reliance on the Holy Spirit is one of the underpinnings of *The Coach Model for Christian Leaders*. It takes you out of having to be the subject matter expert and lets others shine. Using this approach has greatly enhanced our abilities to see leaders grow in confidence and competence. I love it.

Andrea Buczynski
VP, Global Leadership Development, Cru

As a mental health specialist for over 30 years I have read every page of this carefully crafted book on coaching. All the keys to successful coaching are in these pages. You will find it practical, encouraging and very empowering to be at your very best.

Gregory L. Jantz, PhD
Founder, The Center A Place Of HOPE

Keith Webb hits the nail on the head with *The Coach Model for Christian Leaders*. He has learned the hard way—through direct experience and experimentation—what it means to help others draw out their own conclusions rather than your own. Filled with practical examples, Webb's examination of this ready-to-use coaching model exemplifies what it means to move forward while cooperating with the Holy Spirit.

Robert E. Logan
Author of *Coaching 101* and *The Leadership Difference*

The *COACH Model for Christian Leaders* is a must-read for leaders of all shapes and sizes. Keith Webb did a fantastic job providing an incredible resource, jam packed with practical questions, guidance and activities to help leaders become better coaches.

Paul Sohn
Author of *Quarter-Life Calling*

Proverbs 20:5 says "The purposes of a person's heart is like deep waters, but one who has insight draws them out". Keith Webb is a "Person of Insight" and his book *The COACH Model for Christian Leaders* will help you, as it has helped me, to also become a person of insight.

Bob Tiede
LeadingWithQuestions.com and author of
Great Leaders ASK Questions

The COACH Model for Christian leaders is a foundational Christian coaching resource. We use Keith's book as a required text for our nationally accredited coach training in Australia as it provides a well-grounded, people focused and leader friendly book that is easy to understand and grasp. I highly recommend (and do so often) Keith's book to Christian leaders who are wanting to coach, develop and lead others.

Kylie Butler
Managing Director, Christian Coaching Institute, Australia

The Coach Model for Christian Leaders focuses on a simple but robust process to help coaches with their next coaching conversation. Keith Webb is a master communicator and coaching practitioner. Many of our church planter coaches have benefited from Keith's training. And even more have enjoyed this great book, me included!

Dino Senesi
Send Network Coaching Director, Author of
Sending Well: A Field Guide to Great Church Planter Coaching

Keith Webb's heart for coaching was born out of a passion to help leaders fulfill their calling. He is equally passionate about equipping others for the coaching role. *The COACH Model for Christian Leaders* is the fruit of Keith's years of experience in coaching and coach training. Keith is a master in his field—thorough, professional, clear, and inspiring.

Steve Addison
Author of *Movements That Change the World*
Australian Director of MOVE

Keith Webb does an excellent job providing tools that are relevant and effective in *The COACH Model for Christian Leaders*. This book is a must read for the Christian leader desiring to increase their impact and influence.

Eric Peoples
Lead Pastor & Exec Coach, Legacy Church in Farmington, CT

Dr. Webb does a brilliant job weaving together examples, dialogues, comments, principles, and quotes. Further, his self-disclosures and personal writing style set the tone for others to do likewise—to be curious about how they think and act and then to add the personal element of themselves as they connect with others. This newly updated, practical book continues to be highly readable and highly relevant for people at all levels who want to further develop their interpersonal and coaching skills. We highly recommended it for colleagues in Christian ministry and especially for those with member care and leadership responsibilities.

Dr. Kelly O'Donnell and Dr. Michèle Lewis O'Donnell
Consulting Psychologists, Member Care Associates

I know from personal experience that Keith Webb is an effective and compassionate listener, communicator, teacher, and coach. More importantly, he has the ability to convey these skills to Christian business leaders in a variety of fields. Those in leadership positions would be wise to employ his methods and heed his advice.

Steven J. Buri
President, Discovery Institute

The newest edition of *The Coach Model for Christian Leaders* gives greater clarity and tools to the art of coaching. The first edition out-performed all other books in preparing people to be trained as coaches. This edition will prepare and equip, at even a higher level, both the beginner and the skilled coach.

Sam Farina
Director, Assemblies of God Coaching

Keith Webb's book *The Coach Model for Christian Leaders* inspires people to live and lead like Jesus. By creating a conversation that reveals the truth of what is already in the heart of the disciple, the reader learns the necessary skills of being a Holy Spirit led coach. He lays out a foundation, presents effective tools, and sets people up for a thriving coaching business. I highly recommend this book for anyone who leads, coaches, or wants to be a better communicator.

Jill Monaco
President, Jill Monaco Ministries

The Coach Model for Christian Leaders is a practical approach to coach training that produces dramatic results. His method of "asking powerful questions" helps both the coach and the coachee to make better leadership decisions. I highly recommend Keith and his book.

Mitch Maloney
Director, Church of God USA Missions

The Coach Model for Christian Leaders is my go-to resource for my own coaching, as well as for helping others understand what excellent coaching looks like. It is a simple model that has more depth than most I've seen. This is the training we use for our organization. It gives us the tools to be successful in our coaching, and in developing a culture of coaching.

Ray VanGilst
District Superintendent, Christian & Missionary Alliance

Our organization heavily utilize this coaching approach in our line management structure and has embedded it into our culture. All our emerging leaders, member care providers, and departmental heads are required to do coach training and utilize a coaching approach as appropriate. The results have been gratifying.

Peter Smith
Field Ministries Director, World Outreach International

Great coaches come alongside and empower anyone, anywhere, anytime about anything. Keith Webb's book, *The Coach Model for Christian Leaders* blends his expertise, experience and examples in a way that not only explains the heart but the habits of coaching of great coaching. Your equipping journey as a coach can begin here!

Dr. Tim Roehl
Author of *TransforMissional Coaching*

The Coach Model for Christian Leaders is an excellent resource for improving your communication skills. Keith Webb's coaching approach is clear, simple, and easy to follow. It's a great set of tools to help us serve, lead, and shepherd. I heartily recommend this great resource!

Joseph W. Handley
President, Asian Access

As a Christian coach, I coach both church leaders and business people in secular companies. I often suffer from Christianized secular coaching models that basically reduce the quality of the original method. This book is different. *The Coach Model for Christian Leaders* is state of the art from a professional perspective as well as a genuine Christian approach. It lays necessary foundations for the work of a coach and is a practical guide for all who want to coach and empower others to unfold their God-given potential.

Christoph Schalk
Psychologist and Founder of Würzburger Business Coach Akademie

Saturate integrated The COACH Model® as foundational for our coaching cohorts, as well as essential for teaching on how people change. In a world where everyone is piling on more ideas, we need the good news that the Holy Spirit is working in the hearts of people. If we can believe that, we'll begin calling out of others what God is already doing.

David Achata
Director of Coaching, Saturate

Keith Webb's book, *The COACH Model for Christian Leaders,* is an excellent equipping tool! It will enhance the daily conversations you have in ministry and increase your effectiveness in the lives of those you lead."

Bryan Wintersteen
Global Missions Pastor, Briarwood Presbyterian Church

Keith Webb's *The COACH Model for Christian Leaders* links coaching with ministry and real-life experiences. Using stories as examples throughout the book, Keith shares coaching practices, skills and distinctions in a practical and useful way.

Linda J. Miller, MCC
Global Liaison for Coaching at The Ken Blanchard Companies

The COACH Model˙ changed my approach to leadership and equipped me to more effectively develop other leaders.

Félix Ortiz
Staff Care and Development Director, Agape Europe

The
COACH
Model
FOR CHRISTIAN LEADERS

Powerful Leadership Skills
for Solving Problems, Reaching Goals,
and Developing Others

KEITH E. WEBB

NASHVILLE

NEW YORK • LONDON • MELBOURNE • VANCOUVER

The **COACH** Model
FOR CHRISTIAN LEADERS
Powerful Leadership Skills for Solving Problems,
Reaching Goals, and Developing Others

© 2019 **KEITH E. WEBB**

Published in New York, New York, by Morgan James Publishing. Morgan James is a trademark of Morgan James, LLC. www.MorganJamesPublishing.com

The COACH Model® is the registered trademark of Keith E. Webb. Copyright © 2004 Keith E. Webb. Used with permission.

Scriptures taken from the Holy Bible, New International Version®, NIV®. Copyright © 1973, 1978, 1984, 2011 by Biblica, Inc.™ Used by permission of Zondervan. All rights reserved worldwide. www.zondervan.com The "NIV" and "New International Version" are trademarks reg-istered in the United States Patent and Trademark Office by Biblica, Inc.™

ISBN 978-1-64279-357-4 paperback
ISBN 978-1-64279-358-1 eBook
Library of Congress Control Number: 2018913639

Cover Design by:
Rachel Lopez
www.r2cdesign.com

Interior Design by:
Bonnie Bushman
The Whole Caboodle Graphic Design

Morgan James is a proud partner of Habitat for Humanity Peninsula and Greater Williamsburg. Partners in building since 2006.

Get involved today! Visit
www.MorganJamesBuilds.com

For Benjamin and Jessica.

Table of Contents

Preface to the Revised & Expanded Edition

*"Since we live by the Spirit, let us
keep in step with the Spirit."*
—Galatians 5:25

In the 7 years between first publishing *The COACH Model for Christian Leaders* and writing this revised and expanded edition, our team of instructors has trained more than 10,000 Christian leaders how to coach. We've worked with business professionals, ministry leaders, pastors, CEOs, parents, nonprofit workers, managers, supervisors, and volunteers—in more than 30 countries. We've learned a lot about how to help people master coaching skills and put those skills into practice in their work, ministry, and personal lives.

I want to share that know-how with you!

Coaching isn't only a program for your business or organization. It has become an essential set of skills, mindsets, and tools for leaders.

Coaching is an empowering way of communicating by drawing out what God has put in the people with whom you interact.

Conversations form the foundation of everything we do. Your ability to get things done, make changes, or help other people grow depends on the quality of your conversations. If you change your conversations, you'll change your results.

Your ability to get things done, make changes, or help other people grow depends on the quality of your conversations.

The challenge with all how-to books is helping you move from head to hands—to get into action. I expanded each of the chapters that focus on implementing coaching through your day-to-day leadership role. The book was revised to incorporate our newer, more effective ways of teaching the content. These changes have made a big difference to our training participants, so I trust they will for you as well. I also added a sample coaching agreement and two other appendixes to address the steady stream of questions we receive about coaching training, coach certification, and the world's largest coaching association, the International Coach Federation (ICF).

I was tempted to write much more, but the characteristics that made the first edition popular were that it's practical and to the point. In our coaching workshops, I have the time to expand on everything in this book and you have the opportunity to practice it. I hope to meet you there one day.

Keith Webb

Founder & President of Creative Results Management

http://creativeresultsmanagement.com

Foreword

Twenty years ago, Christians were beginning to notice the emergence and relevance of coaching. Apart from the business world, however, few people knew what coaching involved and not much had been written so I decided to write an introductory coaching textbook. I worked on the project for months, reading everything I could find, interviewing successful Christian coaches and drawing on my own training as both a coach and a coachee.

From the beginning, however, I started getting requests for a shorter, more focused, highly practical overview of what coaching is and how it is done. For several years I have been intending to write such a book but not now. Keith Webb has done the job very well and produced a basic primer on coaching for ministry leaders, students and for anyone else who wants to know what coaching is and how it can be applied in our work.

This book brings a fresh perspective, beginning with helpful discussions about coaching mindsets, attitudes and values and ending with guidelines for stepping out and applying coaching to ourselves and to others. In between, the book is filled with practical examples and concise descriptions of coaching skills. The content is summarized concisely in the book's full title: *The COACH Model for Christian*

Leaders: Powerful Leadership Skills for Solving Problems, Reaching Goals, and Developing Others. Keith delivers admirably on the book title's promise.

Unlike others who have written about coaching, Keith draws from his coach training seminars around the world. He has applied the principles described in his book, learned from experience how to teach them to others, and honed his skills and teaching through his work cross-culturally.

Unlike many others, including Christian coaches and trainers, Keith Webb does not buy into the humanistic foundations of the contemporary coaching movement. He makes frequent references to the role of the Holy Spirit in coaching and ties this in to his knowledge of scripture. In doing this, he does not give any watered-down version of coaching. In contrast he presents the core foundations and established principles of coaching and provides an overview that is very consistent with established coaching principles. Throughout the book he shows that "coaching is not about providing answers but about asking thoughtful questions."

Unlike the days when I was writing my book, coaching has become better known and more acceptable. The value of coaching is being demonstrated, experienced and taught by pastors, missionaries, counselors, seminar leaders, and professors in colleges and seminaries. New training programs are making their appearance and books continue to be published, many of which say almost the same thing. Keith Webb's book is different. I know it will appear on the required reading list in the coaching courses that I teach.

I am glad to give my enthusiastic recommendation to *The COACH Model for Christian Leaders* whether you are curious about coaching, a seasoned coach or just getting started.

Gary R. Collins, PhD
Author of *Christian Coaching: Helping Others Turn Potential into Reality*

Coaching Mindsets

"But the Counselor, the Holy Spirit, whom the Father
will send in my name, will teach you all things and
will remind you of everything I have said to you."
—John 14:26

I have a serious illness. It afflicts many without regard to education, economics, or ethnicity. PhDs as well as factory workers suffer from it. It evenly attacks those everywhere—Africa, Asia, Europe, Middle East, and North & South America. People of faith are not immune. In fact, they may have a slightly higher rate of infection, but not by much. Sometimes those with no faith at all can exhibit the strongest symptoms of the illness. There are those who say the illness doesn't exist—or if it does, it only exists in others.

It's called *know-it-all-ism*.

Know-it-all-ism affects the ability of the mind to take in information and process it without prejudice. The illness causes blindness to opinions, answers, and solutions other than their own.

There are two strains of this infection: aggressive and passive. Both strains cause the infected person to believe their ideas are better than others' and that they are correct. The difference between the strains of infection is in how this belief is expressed.

The symptoms of *aggressive know-it-all-ism* are:

- Quick to speak
- Listens until the other person takes a breath
- Has an answer for everything
- Wins arguments, but loses respect

The symptoms of *passive know-it-all-ism* are:

- An appearance of listening
- Maintains a smug facial expression
- Asks questions that subtly point out why the speaker is wrong
- Internally mocks or criticizes the speaker

Do these descriptions bring a couple of people to mind? People afflicted with *know-it-all-ism* are all around us. However, the ability to spot *know-it-all-ism* in others may be a sign that you yourself suffer from this illness. As you continue, try to read for your own benefit rather than for the purpose of fixing others.

Know-It-All-Ism Diagnosed

My first big leadership role began when the organization I worked with in Japan at the time appointed me as the Director of Church Multiplication. I was 28 years old and more than ready to go. I supervised seven American families that were tasked with planting new churches. Due to my illness of *know-it-all-ism*, my communication style relied heavily on advising. I regularly handed out advice in the form of ideas, suggestions, hints, speeches, teaching, and even prayer requests.

As I offered strategies regarding the ministries of the other families, I quickly discovered that my suggestions and help were not always welcomed or appreciated. Like me, they had their own ideas. I was taken aside and talked to several times over those first few years about "pushing my agenda," "running over the feelings of others," and not listening. "We have ideas too," they informed me.

It wasn't just that I was afflicted with *know-it-all-ism*, as a supervisor I also felt responsible for my teammates. I thought if I knew something would be helpful, it was my duty to tell them. To not say something would be irresponsible.

I was puzzled that my efforts to help were perceived as arrogant or dictatorial, and I was frustrated that even after I realized this was happening, I didn't have other communication tools with which to help our group accomplish its goals.

"To improve is to change; to be
perfect is to change often."
—Winston Churchill

Changes in My Thinking

Three things happened that changed not only my communication skills, but also how I thought about leading other people.

First of all, I heard about a set of non-directive communication skills called *coaching* that help people find solutions and grow. Coaching involves listening to others, asking questions to deepen thinking, allowing others to find their own solutions, and doing it all in a way that makes people feel empowered and responsible enough to take action.

The problem was I was terrible at listening and asking questions. I already knew what people should do, or so I thought. Why did I need to ask them questions about things when I already knew the answer?

> "Why do I need to ask questions
> when I already know the answer?"

I was convinced that coaching skills were the key to getting people to accept my ideas and solutions, so I was motivated to learn. However, it didn't feel genuine. I found that bringing others around to my conclusions by using questions was much more difficult than I imagined. (Obviously, I didn't understand coaching.) Some of those I worked with may have felt manipulated, and rightly so. I quickly went back to telling people what I thought they should do. But being a good learner, I renamed my old practice "coaching."[1]

The Holy Spirit

The second thing that helped me change my way of thinking happened when I read a verse in the Gospel of John in which Jesus says this to his disciples,

> *"But the Counselor, the Holy Spirit, whom the Father will send in my name, will teach you all things and will remind you of everything I have said to you" (14:26).*

I was struck by the promise that the Holy Spirit will teach and remind. I thought my job as a leader was to teach and remind. Authority figures in my life had taught and reminded me—parents, teachers, mentors, and supervisors. My church had taught me to teach the truth and to confront error wherever I encountered it.

What did it mean to take Jesus' instruction literally? How can I, as a leader who is responsible for others, not teach or remind?

A short time later, while finishing my master's degree, I took a class with C. Peter Wagner. The class was about church multiplication, and one day Dr. Wagner told the class about the tremendous growth of African independent churches throughout central Africa during the 1980s. He showed graphs that illustrated the dramatic increase in church attendance during that period. Some of the largest churches in the world at that time were to be found in central Africa and were led by African leaders. These churches were not a part of a foreign denomination. Instead they were indigenous.

Someone in the back of the room raised his hand, stood up, and with an emotion-filled voice said, "But Dr. Wagner, some of these churches are largely heretical! Some of those African pastors are corrupt and extremely authoritarian. Their theology is a mix of animistic practices and Christianity. One of the largest of these independent churches doesn't even believe in the deity of Jesus. How can you hold them up as an example of church growth?"

Dr. Wagner smiled and gave a little chuckle, then, stroking his pointy white goatee, he explained that it wasn't until 325 A.D. that the Council of Nicaea agreed on the deity of Jesus, and another 75 years before they could describe the Trinity. It wasn't until the Synod of Hippo in 393 A.D. that the Canon of Scripture as we have it now was settled.

"So," he concluded, "if we can give the Holy Spirit a couple hundred years to work those things out with the early Church leaders, I think we can give Him a couple decades to work out any issues with our African brothers and sisters."

Wow. I was shocked. I bristled and thought this was one of the most irresponsible statements I had ever heard. After all, as ministers, what is our job if it isn't to make sure the Bible is taught and applied correctly? We have the Scriptures, our final authority of faith and action, and if a fellow believer is clearly believing or behaving in non-Biblical ways, shouldn't we confront them with their error? I realized my high view of Scripture was not wrong, but my understanding and reliance on the Holy Spirit was weak.

I also felt convicted. If I was honest, I had to admit I didn't trust the Holy Spirit, and the Holy Spirit alone, to correct any problems in the African church. I incorrectly thought that God needed my help or the help of other Christians. This is surely the height of ministry arrogance. Dr. Wagner, on the other hand, trusted the Holy Spirit to do whatever God wanted without assistance from himself, seminary students, or the American church.

I learned two things about leadership responsibility:

1. It is not my responsibility to change others. The Holy Spirit can and will do it on His own—maybe with me but often without me.
2. It is not my responsibility to correct everything that I think is out of sync with Scripture, company policy, or best practices. The Spirit may choose to use me in this regard, or He may have other means or different timing in mind.

To someone afflicted with *know-it-all-ism* these realizations are nothing short of revolutionary. The pressure I felt to change people decreased, while my reliance on the Holy Spirit to make necessary changes increased. I continued to do my part by speaking up when appropriate, but with an attitude of looking for and joining God in His ongoing work.

The Cost of Advice

The final lesson that solidified my change of mindset happened after my family moved to Indonesia, the largest Muslim country in the world. Once there, I worked with indigenous Christian organizations serving in remote people groups of Indonesia. These groups were Muslim. As you can imagine, the radicals in these areas did not value a free-flow of ideas regarding belief in Jesus, instead they sought to keep out anything they viewed as competing with Islamic dominance. During my years in Indonesia, radicals detonated bombs in Bali and Jakarta, attacked Christian churches, and constantly threatened foreigners.

Against this backdrop, I began working with young Indonesian Christians who were eager to help alleviate poverty, teach children the national language, and to share the good news about Isa al Masih (Jesus the Messiah) with their countrymen. Most of these Indonesian believers were 18- to 21-year-olds with just a high school education and three months of Bible training.

They were eager to learn from me. They appreciated my ideas and wanted more. Even better, I found that they would go and do what I advised them to do. I thought, "Ah, finally someone who will listen to me!" I felt validated, important, and appreciated.

Even though, in my mind at least, I was careful to allow my Indonesian friends to make their own decisions, I gave them a lot of advice. They would go and implement a plan based on my recommendations and then come back to ask for the next steps. I would tell them that they needed to figure it out on their own, but somehow (without too much difficulty) they would get me to give them my advice on their situation. Then they would go do as I had advised.

Here's where my next insight came from. I found that younger Americans, Australians or Europeans, being from egalitarian societies, would listen to me and take whatever part of my advice they found helpful and discard the rest. Indonesia, however, is a socially hierarchical society, where one listens to and follows the advice of someone of a higher status or position. So even though I told them they needed to do it their own way, my Indonesian friends would take my advice quite literally. They believed a good follower does what his or her teacher tells them to do—to not do so would be disrespectful.

One day as I reflected on this situation, I realized that my advice could get these young people killed, beaten, or run out of the villages where they served. Suddenly advice-giving had a huge price tag. Who was I to make life-and-death decisions for these people?

I realized that my advice could get these young people
killed, beaten, or run out of the villages where they served.

It wasn't my place to make these decisions. Each person and team needed to hear from the Holy Spirit regarding his or her next steps. If the Holy Spirit directed them to go somewhere or to do something that resulted in persecution, then that was God's will and He would see them through it. It was critical that they heard from God, not me.

Yet, as a person suffering from *know-it-all-ism* I wasn't equipped with the communication skills necessary to cultivate their ability to hear from the Holy Spirit. I didn't know how to draw out from them what they were hearing and experiencing and help them process all that information into steps that genuinely came from the Spirit.

What was I to do? Then I remembered the non-directive coaching I heard about years earlier. Out of desperation, I began to shift my role from advisor to coach. I focused on listening. I resisted making statements and giving advice. I bought a couple books and wrote down some key questions that I could ask in Indonesian. It was a very difficult process for me. Little by little, however, I made progress.

I write this book as a fellow learner, someone not naturally gifted in listening, asking questions, drawing out, or empowering. I've learned valuable coaching skills that have transformed my interactions with other people. Ideas and advice still come to my mind, but I've learned how to control the urge to tell people what to do and instead, I now can use questions to draw out their thoughts and ideas.

In some ways I'm the last guy that should be writing about coaching skills, because I'm so unnatural at it—and still to this day I am predisposed to offer advice. However, because I'm not natural in these skills, I've had to find ways to learn them.

As my colleagues and I have taught these skills, we've seen thousands of people learn to improve their ability to lead in empowering, non-directive ways by listening, asking questions, and helping people form their own answers rather than providing them.

This process has been a long but incredibly rewarding journey. I hope you'll join me as we take a more in-depth look at what it means to coach others.

What It Really Means To Coach

"The purposes of a person's heart are deep waters,
but one who has insight draws them out."
—Proverbs 20:5

Coaching is like a quest. It is a journey to discover the unknown, and it's the unknown that makes it an adventure. In coaching we embark on a quest by using *questions* in conversations. When you ask coaching questions, you journey to the unknown. It's risky to go on a quest. The unknown plays on our fears as well as our imagination. That can feel uncomfortable. In asking questions, you never know where the answer might take you, because you don't know how the other person will respond.

Not only are you on a quest, the person being asked the questions also embarks on a journey through reflecting on the questions. They discover new things as well. Questions cause people to think in new ways and from new perspectives. We combine several things we often "already knew" and end up in a new place, with new perspective.

Noble quests are for the sake of someone else. Answers should come from the recipient of the question, not the asker. If the asker uses questions to lead the person somewhere, it is not a true quest. Asking questions allows both coach and coachee to journey into the unknown to discover what God has prepared.

Why All The Confusion About Coaching?

There's a lot of confusion about what exactly coaching is and how to effectively coach. Coaching is an unregulated field. Anyone can, and many do, call themselves a coach.

A friend of mine met a woman at a party who said she was a Life Coach. My friend asked her, "Where did you train to be a Life Coach?" The woman answered, "Well, in life!" As a Professional Certified Coach and coach instructor, I groan when I hear this response because without special coaching training, rather than asking questions in a discovery process, she most likely gives her clients advice about their lives. The popular image of a Life Coach, and many sports coaches for that matter, is pretty much the opposite of what coaching has become.

Coaching isn't about teaching someone what we know.
Coaching is about helping people to learn.

The largest coaching association in the world is the International Coach Federation (ICF). The ICF has established a body of best practices that define what effective coaching is and isn't. The type of coaching you'll learn in this book, while built from a distinctly Christian theology and worldview and tested in ministry since 2004, aligns with the ICF.

Coaching Defined

How you define coaching reveals much about the values, mindset, and approach you bring to working with other people. You will act in accordance with your beliefs. In this book, I define coaching by its practice and its results:

Coaching is an ongoing intentional conversation that empowers a person or group to fully live out God's calling.

Let's pull this definition apart and take a look at each concept.

Coaching is an ongoing...

If you use coaching skills as part of your everyday leadership, coaching will increase the effectiveness of your one-time, short, spontaneous conversations. For much deeper transformation, coaching is most successful over a period of time, through regular interactions. Many leaders choose to coach for 30-minutes to an hour every two weeks over a period of several months, or on-the-job through short conversations throughout the week. The regularity of coaching conversations makes a huge impact on your results.

...intentional conversation...

"Intentional" does not refer to a pre-determined outcome. Every conversation is expected to produce Spirit-led discoveries, insights, and action steps. A coaching methodology utilizes processes and communication skills designed to keep the coachee in the driver's seat reflecting on ideas, making decisions, and taking action. It takes intentionality to have this kind of conversation with people.

...that empowers...

The overall result of a coaching conversation is that the coachee feels empowered. She has grown. She feels more equipped to think through and handle situations on her own. Throughout the coaching relationship, she has set the agenda for each conversation, created her own action steps, and made her own decisions. There is no manipulation or dependency on the coach. In this sense, coaching is developmental. Coachees learn how to learn, think critically, and make good decisions.

...a person or group...

Coaching focuses on an individual's reflection, growth, and forward action. Groups can also be coached. A group of people with the same goals can be coached simultaneously. Each person will learn from the coaching interaction of the others. Teams can also be coached around the team's goals and each person's contribution toward those goals. In the case of teams, the personal growth needs of each team member would require individual coaching.

...to fully live out...

Coaching helps people to thrive, excel and to live out their full potential, rather than just making do. The process of coaching encourages greater obedience to God and alignment with His desires.

...God's calling.

Here is where my definition diverges from many others—both secular and Christian. I believe that a coach's job involves more than just helping another person to achieve whatever he or she wants. The coach and coachee must also pay attention to God's larger purposes. Coaches help people to become what God would have them become (Ephesians 1:4, 5), and to do what God would have them do (Ephesians 2:10).

Coaching supports and encourages the calling, gifting, and unique potential that God has given each person. Calling is discovered and clarified by many different means throughout a person's life. A coach is only one of many people who is able to help discern God's call on a person's life. Throughout the coaching process, the coach seeks to help the coachee clarify what God is saying to him or her and assist them in discerning what it means to live that out.

What Does A Coach Do?

To most leaders, coaching practices are counter-intuitive. Many people see coaching as just another term for teaching one-on-one. One recent study found that managers think they are coaching when they are actually just telling people what to do. Even more worrisome is their peers reinforced their "micromanaging-as-coach" as good coaching.[2] The good news is, with some training and practice, leaders can learn coaching skills and experience better results.

Take a look at these fundamental characteristics of good coaching.

- Coaches don't talk, they listen.
- Coaches don't give information, they ask questions.
- Coaches don't offer ideas, they generate ideas from coachees.
- Coaches don't share their story, they tap into the coachee's experience.
- Coaches don't present solutions, they expand the coachee's thinking.
- Coaches don't give recommendations, they empower coachees to choose.

Many leaders reading this list for the first time, scratch their heads and say, "Huh?" Yet, this is a basic description of what professional coaches do and don't do.

---

*To most leaders, professional coaching practices
are counter-intuitive, and that's good!*

Coaching—Three "Sets"

Coaching draws from many disciplines and integrates a number of approaches to working with people. A professional coach has mastered three "sets": a coaching mindset, a coaching skill set, and a coaching tool set. Each element in these sets are not unique to coaching, however, the way coaches combine the elements creates a unique, counter-intuitive, approach to helping people make changes in their lives.

These three coaching "sets" come from the best practices of professional coaches. You might not want to become a coach as a role but learning best practices for coaching will help you lead more effectively in any leadership role. (More on integrating coaching skills into your various leadership roles in the next chapter.)

Learning and using these three coaching "sets" will produce lasting results and develop the coachee's capacity to solve other problems and reach other goals on their own.

1. **Coaching mindset.** Coaching requires a number of mindset shifts from some of the ways we usually think about helping people. For example, a coach doesn't provide their answers, a coach draws out answers from their coachees. This mindset shift is essential for those who want to coach well. Here are a few more:
   - Asking questions will generate better learning—for you and your coachees.
   - Your information isn't necessary—coachees need perspective, focus, and courage.

- Discovery is far more powerful than you telling coachees something.
- Internal change is transformational and produces fundamental solutions to problems.
- It's not about you and what you have to offer, it's about your coachees.

2. **Coaching skill set.** For leaders who are accustomed to talking, offering solutions, and sharing their experience, the biggest challenge is to stop talking. When we do, we find it difficult to ask questions because, frankly, we're not very good at it. Our curiosity is limited because we think we already know the answer. We know how to talk, but not to ask. Professional coaches rely on these skills:
   - Active listening so others can express themselves.
   - Asking powerful questions that initiate a change of thinking.
   - Generating feedback that avoids defensiveness.
   - Expanding awareness that creates new learning.
   - Designing action steps that will actually be accomplished.
   - Following-up to increase learning and accountability.

Excellent coaching means mastering 3 sets: a coaching mindset, a coaching skill set, and a coaching tool set.

---

3. **Coaching tool set.** Coaching is a learning process, not a teaching process. Many of the teaching tools we regularly use can't be used in coaching. Professional coaches have a different set of tools. These tools flow from a coaching mindset and use a coaching skill set in order to facilitate the coachee's learning.

- Conversational learning processes, such as The COACH Model®.
- Processes to discover the most relevant topic for each coaching conversation.
- Tools to focus on the person, not the problem.
- Techniques to identify and challenge limiting beliefs.
- Patterns of internal barriers.
- Grids to assist coachees to make sound decisions.
- Tools to get people into action.

These descriptions of what it really means to be a coach focus on the processes professional coaches use to help people change in order to solve their problems and reach their goals. The thing is, the results would be different if you used a different process.

For example, if you took a consultative approach and prepared solutions for the coachee, it might produce a good result. But that result would be different than if you coached the coachee to find his own solutions. With a coaching approach, the coachee may identify internal barriers in themselves and their organization. They may explore solutions that flow from the experience, strengths, and passion of their team. And they will most certainly own and feel more responsible for the solutions because of the coaching process.

The Holy Spirit, The Body of Christ, And Coaching

Christians, like many other people, love to teach, advise, and correct. I believe we overuse these activities. This habit comes from an incomplete understanding of the roles of the Holy Spirit and the Body of Christ, and a lack of non-directive communication skills.

In the first chapter, I shared with you my understanding of the Holy Spirit and His perfect ability to teach and remind both the coach and the coachee. Let's take a deeper look.

All Christians have the Holy Spirit inside them. Jesus sent believers a Counselor (John 14:15-18) to teach and remind (John 14:26). Christian coaches are not a substitute for the Holy Spirit. In our efforts to help, this is easy to forget. Our knowledge, experience, intuition, and spiritual discernment can tempt us to move to conclusions and lead us to believe we know what the other person needs. More important than the coach's perspective is the Holy Spirit's perspective, and how He is leading the other person.

A basic and Biblical assumption is that God is already at work in the life of the person we are coaching.

> "Jesus said to them, 'My Father is always at his work to this very day, and I, too, am working.' 'I tell you the truth, the Son can do nothing by himself; he can do only what he sees his Father doing…'" (John 5:17, 19b).

If Jesus could do nothing by Himself, then how much more should we abandon our agendas, strategies, and plans for the other person and, instead, join the Father in His work in and through him or her? He will continue to work in the coachee, with or without us. As Paul wrote, "… He who began a good work in you will carry it on to completion until the day of Christ Jesus" (Philippians 1:6). One key to effective coaching is for the coachee and coach to understand what God is doing and join His work.[3]

Coaching integrates a discernment process. All believers have the Holy Spirit, but not all believers listen to His voice and know how to respond well. Learning to listen to the Holy Spirit is essential to understanding God's will. The coach's job is to encourage the other person to reflect, to seek the Holy Spirit, and to hear His voice. In this task, a coach is similar to a good spiritual director. Richard Foster writes, "What is the purpose of a spiritual director? … His direction is simply and clearly to lead us to our real director. He is the means of God to open the path to the inward teaching of the Holy Spirit."[4]

Every believer has the Holy Spirit and thus a direct link to God without a human priest mediator (Hebrews 10:19-20). Spiritual discernment, however, is a social, not individualistic process. God created the Body of Christ as a social setting where His will is made known, interpreted, and applied (1 Corinthians 12:12-30). A person outside an active role in the Body of Christ cannot fully understand and apply God's will in his or her own life. We mature through our interaction within the Body of Christ (Ephesians 4:11-16).

Spiritual discernment is a social, not individualistic process.

Coaching can play an important role in helping people think through how they process their spiritual discernment and how they might involve the appropriate members of the Body of Christ in that process. Consider the relational nature of humans, "*Persona* in Latin comes from the Greek word *prosopon*, which can be translated 'face to face.' Each human is a person as he or she stands face to face, turned toward another person, engaged in dialogue, involved in relationship. We discover our personhood in community, in relationship."[5]

In coaching, we acknowledge that the coachee has many other people involved in his or her life. These people are a rich resource that we need to encourage the coachee to draw from. The coach should never view himself or herself as anyone's sole source of help.

Process Versus Content

To understand coaching well, it is helpful to distinguish between Process and Content. The Content of a coaching conversation includes the topic of the conversation, facts, information, ideas, and commitments. The Process includes how the coach and coachee go about discussing and working with the Content.

The responsibility for Process and Content is not equally divided in coaching. This lack of balance is not typical of other types of

CONTENT AND PROCESS IN COACHING	
Content	**Process**
• Topic, goal, problem. • Stories, facts, information. • Ideas, options, action steps. • Insights, decisions, commitments.	• Establishes trust. • Monitors physical setting and emotional safety. • Draws out thoughts and ideas. • Listens actively, clarifies, and summarizes. • Asks questions to evoke discovery. • Challenges appropriately. • Co-creates plans of action. • Follows-up plans for accountability and learning.
Content is primarily the coachee's responsibility.	*Process is primarily the coach's responsibility.*

Table 1

conversations—and this is what makes coaching so powerful. In a friendship, conversation Content is provided by each individual in a fairly balanced manner—each person shares his or her stories, ideas, suggestions, and advice. If you are in a teaching role, you may be responsible for both the Process and Content.

The coach does not provide Content: the information, ideas, or recommendations. In coaching, the coach focuses almost entirely on the Process, drawing out nearly all the Content from within the coachee.

In Table 1, notice the verbs at the beginning of each Process statement. Process is mostly about atmosphere and conversation dynamics. The coach is largely responsible for the Process. All of the Process is directed toward helping the coachee make discoveries, find solutions, and move forward in terms of understanding and action. As a coach focuses on Process the coachee will find his or her own answers.

Share Questions, Not Content

My schools, university, and seminary trained me to teach, propose ideas, and find solutions. All Content. So, when someone brings a problem to me, my first impulse is to share my ideas on how to solve it. I was trained to provide answers (Content), not to help people find their own solutions (Process).

In later chapters I will go into more detail on how to ask powerful questions. For right now, let me say that asking questions is an excellent method for helping the other person listen to the Holy Spirit. Questions naturally draw Content from the coachee. Questions cause the person to look within, look up, and look around for the answers.

The examples below illustrate different things that come up in conversations. The first sentence demonstrates how we might be tempted to share our Content, and the second sentence gives an example of a

Process question that's directed towards drawing Content from the other person.

Re: Topic
Content Statement: Today we are going to work on your character.
Process Question: What result would you like from our conversation?

Re: Stories
Content Statement: Here's how I handled that situation.
Process Question: How have you handled this type of situation in the past?

Re: Facts
Content Statement: There are three things you need to know about this.
Process Question: What is important for you to know about this?

Re: Information
Content Statement: I can give you a good book on that topic.
Process Question: Where could you find the information you need?

Re: Ideas
Content Statement: How about a huge poster in the shape of a monkey?
Process Question: What ideas do you have?

Re: Suggestions
Content Statement: If I were you, I would sit him down and tell him everything.
Process Question: What options do you see?

Re: Insights

Content Statement: I think you are realizing that more self-discipline is needed here.

Process Question: What insights occur to you?

Re: Action Steps

Content Statement: Here's what I want you to do before next week.

Process Question: What will you do to move forward?

Re: Decisions

Content Statement: You should do that.

Process Question: What decisions do you need to make?

The power of coaching is in the Process. A coach empowers others by helping them to self-discover, gain clarity and awareness, as well as by drawing Content from them. A good coach draws out what the Holy Spirit has put in.

A good coach draws out what the Holy Spirit has put in.

Learning Without Teaching

Does coaching really work? Can you actually help someone without giving them ideas, suggestions, or advice based on your own experience? Yes! And this is why coaching is so exciting. You don't have to have answers for other people, you simply assist them in thinking about their situation and allow the Holy Spirit to work through your questions and their answers.

Here's an example of a conversation that illustrates how a coach used Process to help a coachee discover the Content he needed to move forward. Notice how the coach doesn't give advice, but simply asks meaningful questions to help the coachee learn something new.

Nick asked to be coached on how to restore his relationship with his Czech ministry partner. Nick had lived in the Czech Republic for seven years, and he was partnering with Jiri, a young Czech pastor.

The first year of ministry together went well. In the second year, tensions steadily increased between the two men. Nick complained that Jiri was making decisions by himself and ignored his input. The church hadn't grown as they anticipated, and instead of trying the many ideas Nick suggested, Jiri seemed to give up, spending more and more time in sermon preparation.

The coach asked how Nick had approached this situation with Jiri. On several occasions, Nick had spoken directly with Jiri about the tensions, apologized for his part, and gently gave Jiri feedback on his own behavior. Jiri suggested that if Nick didn't like how things were going, he should consider moving back to Prague and rejoining his mission organization's efforts there. Nick was shocked and hurt.

Having heard about Nick's efforts to resolve the conflict, the coach asked a question that he himself did not know the answer to. He asked, "How do Czech's resolve conflict?" Nick started to answer, and then thought for a moment, "I'm not sure, actually."

"Would that be something worth finding out?" his coach asked.

"Sure, but I have no idea how." Nick responded.

The coach asked, "Where could you find that information?"

"I've got a couple books on Czech culture, but I don't think there's much there on conflict resolution."

"How else could you find out?"

He thought for a moment, "I suppose I could talk with Pastor Horsky. He's got to be 70 years old and is the Czech version of Billy Graham. I interviewed him for a research project I did two years ago for my master's degree, he was very helpful."

"Excellent. Who else might be helpful?"

"Our mission's field director has been here since the fall of communism. I could call him."

"Alright. Anyone else?"

"I know a sociology professor from the University. He attended English classes here at the church last year. I could meet him for coffee." With that, Nick had his plan for researching Czech conflict resolution.

Two weeks later, Nick came back with a three-page summary of not only how Czechs resolve conflict, but also how leader-subordinate relationships function in Czech culture.

Nick realized that his approaches to resolving the conflict had actually made things worse, pushing Jiri to become more defensive and distant.

Armed with his learning on Czech conflict resolution, Nick patiently applied these new concepts as he worked on his relationship with Jiri over the next four months. They turned a corner, and the two men continued to work well together for the next three years.

Questions are powerful tools to help people gain new awareness and shift perspective. The question, "How do Czechs resolve conflict?" raised Nick's awareness. The coach didn't know the answer, and neither did Nick. The question was purely serendipitous. It shifted the discussion from Nick's efforts and Jiri's resistance, which were symptoms of the problem, to deeper underlying cultural differences. The question prompted Nick to explore further, which resulted in deep learning. The experience also equipped Nick in *how* he can learn new things on his own from the resources (people and information) around him in the Czech Republic.

Questions are powerful tools to help people
gain new awareness and shift perspective.

Action-Reflection Cycle

Every day we have dozens of experiences that are new or are, in some big or small way, different from those we have previously encountered. However, we often do not stop and reflect on these experiences, so we miss out on the benefits that they provide. We fail to learn from them. Some experiences provide models that we want to continue following and others provide warnings to avoid in the future.

Coaching is an application of the Action-Reflection Cycle. At a human-level, the world operates through a complex chain of cause and effect. Many times, we lose track of the effects of our actions as they move through the cause and effect chain further and further away from what began it. If we can understand the effects of our actions (or inaction), we can use that greater clarity and understanding to further adjust our thinking and behavior and produce further improvements. If we fail to learn from our experiences, we can end up repeating avoidable and costly mistakes.

Acting, then reflecting on the effect, then adjusting the action is called *single-loop learning*.[6] It is the simplest form of the Action-Reflection Cycle. This kind of learning is based on performing a number of similar, yet improved, actions. Even though some additional improvement can be achieved, this level of reflection doesn't often

THE ACTION REFLECTION CYCLE

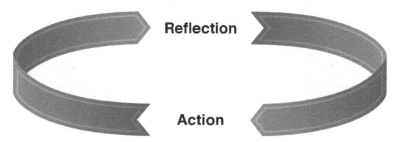

Figure 1: The Action-Reflection Cycle

result in innovative breakthroughs. Without someone or something else to stimulate our thinking, we tend to remain in the "more of the same" type reflection. It's easy to get stuck in a fixed pattern. This is when coaching can help.

Coaching enhances the Action-Reflection Cycle by encouraging a person to reflect beyond incremental improvements to the current actions. Coaching around the coachee's assumptions, goals, and meaning can provide a new perspective and lead to a breakthrough. This is called *double-loop learning*. The coachee acts and observes the results. Then rather than simply adjusting the original action to improve it, they step back and reflect on the broader assumptions that led them to that action in the first place. Changes at the assumption level can produce significant differences and will automatically produce ideas for new actions, producing different and hopefully better results. These results can then be used to review and perfect the strategy or reexamine the assumptions further.

Throughout this book you will find different techniques and processes to help others to examine their assumptions and beliefs so that they can see their situation from different perspectives. As coachees intentionally engage in the Action-Reflection Cycle they can make life-changing progress toward their goals.

The COACH Model®

I've shared with you the theory behind coaching. Now let me introduce you to the practice through the acronym C.O.A.C.H.

The COACH Model® follows a pattern that has proven to produce successful, holistic, and empowering conversations. It harnesses the power of the Action-Reflection Cycle and creates a flexible conversation guide that allows the coachee to reach significant milestones that produce insight, learning, and responsible forward movement.

Why Do We Need A Model For A Conversation?

Let me share two stories that illustrate how people bring different strengths to conversations, but those strengths also have weaknesses associated with them.

Wendy shared with me about her conversations with a neighbor who was involved in a difficult marriage. Wendy listened well and was very empathic. The neighbor felt heard and cared for but didn't seem to change or move forward. Week after week the neighbor brought the same problems. Wendy wondered how she could adjust the conversation to help her neighbor take some kind of action toward a more satisfying marriage.

A man I know was notorious, according to his wife and co-workers, for immediately offering solutions whenever he heard a problem. In his mind, if a person chose to share a problem with him, then obviously they expected him to suggest a solution. He thought he was being helpful. Others felt the opposite about his responses. They thought he didn't listen, wasn't empathetic, and didn't care about them.

Each of these two people were strong in different parts of the conversation process. Wendy was an excellent empathic listener and needed to learn how to help people move toward action. My other friend jumped straight to action steps and needed to learn to listen, explore, and help people make discoveries that will lead to their own solutions. The COACH Model® helps both of these types of people to grow in the areas in which they are not naturally gifted.

Coaching isn't about providing answers,
it's about asking thought-provoking questions.

The COACH Model® is pure Process. The Content, the destination and discoveries along the way are determined completely by the person being coached. Many people find that this model gives them the confidence to coach anyone through whatever it is that they want to work on. It's important to remember that coaching isn't about providing answers, it's about asking thought-provoking questions.

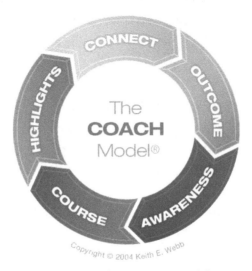

Figure 2: The COACH Model®

The COACH Model® is powered by questions. In the following chapters each step of The COACH Model® is paired with question-asking techniques designed to equip you to ask powerful and helpful questions.

The five steps of the model spell out the word "coach."

1. **C is for Connect:** Connect has two parts. First, connecting with the person you are talking with to build rapport and trust; and second, following-up on action steps from your previous coaching conversation.

2. **O is for Outcome:** Outcome is the intended result the coachee would like to achieve during the conversation. Knowing the outcome at the beginning helps focus the conversation on that which is important to the coachee.

3. **A is for Awareness:** Awareness is a reflective dialogue intended to produce discoveries, insights, and increased perspective for the coachee. The more perspective the coachee has, the more holistically and therefore creatively, he or she will view his or her situation. The coachee will see a greater number of options and, in the end, will make better decisions.

4. **C is for Course:** Course puts feet to insights and discoveries by helping the coachee create action steps. Helping people move into action is an essential part of the coaching experience.

5. **H is for Highlights:** Highlights focus on reviewing the parts of the conversation that the coachee found most meaningful. As the coachee reviews the conversation, they reinforce insights and important points thus strengthening their learning. Highlights also reveal to the coach how the coachee benefited from the conversation.

The remainder of this book explains each step of The COACH Model® and inserts appropriate listening, questioning, and processing skills along the way.

Before moving to The COACH Model® and teaching you coaching mindsets, skills, and tools, it would first be good to address how you can broadly apply this book in all your leadership roles.

Coaching As A Way Of Leading

"Jesus called them together and said, 'You know that those who are regarded as rulers of the Gentiles lord it over them, and their high officials exercise authority over them. Not so with you. Instead, whoever wants to become great among you must be your servant, and whoever wants to be first must be slave of all. For even the Son of Man did not come to be served, but to serve, and to give his life as a ransom for many.'"
—Mark 10:42-45

J esus described leadership as serving people rather than lording over them. Two thousand years later— even after all the "How to Be An Empowering Leader" workshops—we still struggle with autocratic leadership. Leaders, in Jesus' day as well as ours, determine the direction of the organization and assign tasks because of their authority.

Those leaders who assign tasks arbitrarily or for their own personal gain "lord over" their followers. In contrast to this way of leading, Robert Greenleaf coined the term "servant leadership." Service to others, rather than control, distinguishes servant leaders. Coaching, rather than directing, is an excellent way to serve others. As leaders adopt a coaching approach, they become less autocratic and more empowering, a servant leader.

Coaching can be used much more than only through formal coaching conversations. You can and should integrate coaching skills into your various leadership roles.

Leaders Must Do More Than Be Directive

Leadership professor J Robert Clinton defines leadership as influence. If you influence others, you are leading, regardless of the position you hold. Some leaders are recognized, and many are not. Everyone has influence, the question is, how are you using that influence?

People with leadership positions can use their authority to "force" others, rather than finding ways to draw out natural abilities, interests, and motivations. As you read this, dictators and conscienceless-business people may come to mind, but what about parents, supervisors, and pastors who use their authority, or spiritual authority in the case of pastors, to "force" people to behave certain ways?

We "force" people to do things when we have authority and tell people what to do and how to do it. They may not like it, but they don't say anything because of the authority we hold over them. No wonder staying engaged at work is a struggle for many employees.

I want to give you a new set of tools that will help you lead and communicate in new ways. If you change your conversations, you will change your results. This principle holds true in your work, at home, with your spouse, kids, co-workers, and customers. If you change your conversations with them, you will change your results with them.

If you change your conversations, you will change your results.

Think of a scale of communication styles (see Table 2). At one end are all the "telling" approaches—teaching, preaching, and advising. Most of us are well-trained and skilled on this end of the scale. The other end of the communication scale is "drawing out" by asking questions and listening. I'm naturally weak with these skills. And I'm not alone. We train thousands of leaders every year in coaching skills. Few say they are natural in drawing out skills, yet all want to learn.

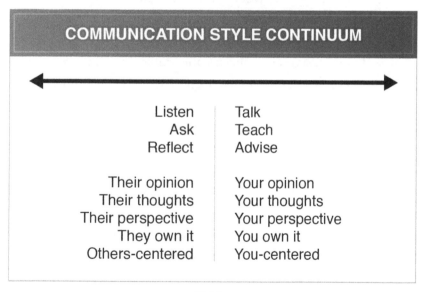

COMMUNICATION STYLE CONTINUUM

Listen	Talk
Ask	Teach
Reflect	Advise
Their opinion	Your opinion
Their thoughts	Your thoughts
Their perspective	Your perspective
They own it	You own it
Others-centered	You-centered

Table 2

The advantages and disadvantages of the "Telling" end of the scale are well-known. The advantages of the "Drawing out" end are not often emphasized. If you ask questions and listen to people, they will share their opinions, thoughts, and perspectives. When they do so, what they say flows out of who they are, their personality, their culture, their life experience, and their interests. What you tell someone might work for you, but they're a different person. If we help a person discover something for themselves, they will own it.

As I share with you about coaching, I want to be clear, I'm not suggesting that you should stop teaching, preaching, sharing your wisdom, disciplining your children, or giving your opinion. Not at all. You have an obligation to function in these ways in many situations. Too many of us, however, rely on these "telling" approaches almost exclusively. They are the only tools in our leadership toolbox. I want to give you some new tools to communicate by drawing out from other people. It will change your relationships and your results.

Distinguishing Leadership Roles and Style

After leading workshops for ministry and marketplace leaders for more than a dozen years, I've learned that people have difficulty distinguishing between a leadership role and a leadership style.

A leadership role often includes a number of responsibilities. Then there's leadership style, which are the ways the leader interacts with people and does his or her work.

The savvy leader has the ability to use a variety of leadership styles depending on the situation and the specific interaction within their leadership role. Poor leaders get stuck in only one style of interaction. Like the supervisor who is constantly directive, telling employees how to do their jobs. Or the Pastor who overly relies on teaching, turning all conversations into a mini seminar rather than listening and drawing out reflection from other people.

Parents confuse their role with leadership styles as well. We want our children (especially teenagers) to like us, hang out with us, and talk to us. So, we try to relate to them as Friends. That is, until the kids want to do something we don't approve of, and we quickly change back to the Parent role and say no. This same dynamic happens with Supervisors.

I'm your Friend or your supportive Consultant until you want to do your work differently than I want it done, then I switch back to your Supervisor. Changing leadership roles confuses those who follow you.

You can't easily change your *role* with people, but you can use different *styles* of interaction with them. In fact, great leaders have an array of leadership tools and approaches they call upon depending on the situation and need.

Coaching Is Both A Role And A Style of Leading

Coaching is a mindset, skill set, and tool set that can be integrated into your various leadership roles. You might be a Pastor, Supervisor, Business Owner, Parent, Disciple-Maker, or Friend. In each of these roles you cannot coach one hundred percent of the time. You have other responsibilities in your role. But you can integrate some coaching practices into your leadership roles. Adding a coaching style of interaction is essential for you to be the most effective you can be, regardless of the role.

In the role of Coach, I one hundred percent coach people. I don't advise them. I don't tell them my ideas, stories, or teach them. I ask questions and listen deeply to help them reflect and find answers they are committed to.

I also have other leadership roles. I'm the President of my organization. I'm also a Trainer, Public Speaker, and Consultant at times. Personally, I'm a Friend, Son, Husband, Father, and Disciple-Maker. I've learned to integrate coaching skills into each of these roles to be a more effective leader.

For example, I'm a Parent to two young adult children. I cannot and shouldn't be 100% Coach for them. My responsibilities as a Parent require me to be very directive with them, at times. It's not wise for me to be directive *all the time*. Not as a Parent. Not as a Supervisor. Not as a Disciple-Maker. Not in any of my leadership roles.

At times, you must be directive in your leadership role, but that doesn't have to be your default style.

Coaching As A Parent Or A Supervisor

As my kids reached their teen years, I increased the amount of listening and questions I used when interacting with them. I chose a more coaching style of communication with them when I could. I held off on giving them my advice more than I did when they were younger. I first found out what they wanted and valued before communicating what I wanted for them. At the same time, I didn't abdicate my role as Parent. I was still directive when it was needed. As a result, I showed them the respect for their independence that they wanted from me and our relationship remained strong during these transitional years.

Great leaders have an array of leadership tools and approaches they call upon, depending on the situation and need.

The role of Supervisor is broad. Supervisors have authority over other people. They manage, support, and hold employees accountable for organizational goals and standards. Their role requires being directive at times, but not nearly as much as is often practiced.

Integrating coaching skills into Supervision as a leadership style is a great way for Supervisors to empower and develop employees. This doesn't mean the supervisor suddenly becomes a non-directive Coach. No, the supervisor uses coaching skills while maintaining their authority.

Take, for example, setting the agenda for a discussion. Tell the employee what you want to talk with him or her about, then ask, "And what would you like to make sure we cover?" Ask a couple clarifying questions about their answer. Asking these questions shows respect and draws out the employee's interests and needs. This is essentially the Outcome process that I'll teach in chapter 5.

Here's a different example, something I did recently. Before jumping in and re-explaining something to a confused employee, I asked, "What part are you not clear about?" Then I addressed just that part, rather than boring and belittling her by re-explaining the whole process, much of which she was clear on.

There is a common tension that leaders experience. It feels easier and faster to lead from our authority, so we over-rely on advising, telling, and directing. In doing so, we do not release the gifting, calling, and creativity that God has built into the people we lead.

The great news is, you can benefit from coaching skills, even if you're not in the role of Coach. I've learned to integrate coaching skills into all my leadership roles as a style of leading.

As you read this book, look for what you can integrate into your various leadership roles. Look for individual mindsets, skills, questions, or tools. Don't worry about trying to adopt the whole coaching approach in your leadership roles. Use what you can, when you can.

At the same time, I want to encourage you to try out the role of Coach with a few people. Learning to coach means unlearning many other habits. If you practice coaching in conversations where you expect yourself to be 100% Coach, you'll find it easier to stick to a coaching approach. After you become skilled at coaching as a result of this focused practice, you will find it easier to then integrate more and more coaching into your other leadership roles.

Connect

> *"My dear brothers and sisters, take note of this: Everyone should be quick to listen, slow to speak and slow to become angry..."*
> —James 1:19

The first step of The COACH Model® is to Connect. The purpose of connecting is to begin the coaching conversation on an informal and personal note that helps to re-establish rapport since the previous conversation.

A bit of chit-chat at the beginning of the conversation helps you and the person you are coaching to connect and engage. Most people will naturally begin conversations this way. However, once a coaching relationship is established, it's not uncommon to jump immediately to the topic at hand and forget the "small talk." Small it may be, but it is talk with a purpose.

Trust is Felt

One time when I lived in Tokyo, I stopped a man to ask for directions. He thought and looked around, hesitated, and finally gave me directions, pointing me up the street to the left. His response did not give me much confidence in his information. Shortly afterward, I spotted an information counter just inside a department store. I asked the young woman for directions to the same location. She confidently told me to go back the way I had come, past the train station, and after a couple of blocks, I would arrive at my destination. I did not have a relationship with either person, but after a brief interaction with each of them, I trusted the young woman's directions. Trust develops out of the rapport that we sense with others.

Trust in the other person also governs our conversations. Think of a time when you had a conversation with someone whom you knew and trusted. Now, contrast that experience with a time when you conversed with someone you did not trust. While the content of the conversation could be exactly the same, our view of the other person affects the results.

How Much Trust Is Needed?

The way in which we interact with people requires differing levels of trust. Consider two people who want to help you using different approaches. One person gives you guidance and advice on your problem. He shares from his knowledge and experience and tells you what he knows on the subject. Now, imagine a second person that helps you by listening and asking good questions. She does not share advice, instead she draws out your ideas and then helps you sharpen and improve them.

Here's the question: which helper do you need to trust more in order to utilize their help?

Most people feel they need to trust the first person. The reason is, if we don't trust the person, we can't trust their guidance and advice. In this case, the person helping is seen as an expert who must be "qualified" through their background and their relationship to us. Yet, does having a strong, trustworthy relationship with the person actually make the advice any better than if there wasn't a strong relationship? No, but it makes the advice easier to accept.

Think of the second approach, where the person helping primarily listens and asks questions. Trust is important and so is relationship, however, the levels of trust and relationship can be quite different if all the ideas and solutions are your own, instead of the helper's. It takes far less relational history to accept help from someone who asks questions and listens.

It takes far less relational history to accept help
from someone who asks questions and listens.

How Coaching Builds Trust

The nature of the conversation and the technique the coach uses helps facilitate trust. Let's look at what builds trust, rapport, and shows respect.

A coaching approach builds trust by:

- Supporting rather than controlling
- Encouraging ideas rather than sharing them
- Yielding responsibility rather than taking it
- Processing decisions rather than making them
- Believing in the person rather than trying to fix them
- Keeping appointments and honoring confidentiality

When a conversation comes from a place of trust and respect, people are engaged and ready to explore, learn and grow. These attitudes and actions hold true throughout the coaching relationship. The Connect stage gives an intentional pause at the beginning of a conversation to allow the coach and coachee to engage together relationally before diving into the goals or problems they wish to work on.

The Power of Small Talk

Let me explain how the Connect step developed. After just a few meetings, coaching conversations begin to develop a rhythm. Both parties know that they are working together through conversations every couple of weeks over the period of several months to solve problems and achieve larger goals. With this sort of rhythm, even after two weeks, it's easy to jump back in where the conversation left off at the last appointment.

Tim and his coach had been coaching together for several months, working mainly on how to transform Tim's team into a cohesive group for the purpose of achieving some pretty aggressive goals.

Tim and his coach met at their normal hour. "Hey coach," Tim said.

The coach jumped right in, "Hi Tim. Are you ready to start?"

"Sure," he replied.

"What progress did you make on your action steps?" the coach asked.

Tim explained what he had done, and they talked about what he learned from it. The coach then asked Tim, "We've been working on bringing your team together around three big goals, what would you see as the next step in accomplishing this?"

Tim shared his thoughts, they identified the specific topic to guide their conversation and went on to coach around that topic for the next 45 minutes. When it came time to create action steps, Tim was unusually reluctant. So, the coach asked him about it, and Tim replied, "Yeah, I'm just not sure if I'll have time to do anything over the next two weeks."

This was surprising. Action steps are key to coaching, and Tim had been very enthusiastic in the past. "What's taking up your time?" his coach asked.

Quietly Tim replied, "My wife was diagnosed with breast cancer two days ago and she's checking into the hospital tomorrow for a series of tests. I'm just not sure I can work on team goals this week."

The coach's jaw dropped in disbelief. Questions ran through his mind: Cancer? How could something so big in Tim's life not come up in the past hour's conversation? What kind of caring coach was he?

Replaying the previous hour in his mind, the coach realized that they had just jumped right in where they had left off from the last coaching conversation and had continued to work on improving Tim's team dynamics. That was their pattern and their purpose for meeting together.

The coach felt sick to his stomach. He was shocked that their so-called personalized coaching hadn't immediately surfaced something as important and personal as Tim's wife's cancer diagnosis.

On reflection, one simple question could have given Tim the opportunity to share about his wife's cancer. "How are you?"

Maybe he would have chosen not to talk about it. Maybe he would have wanted to continue working on his team and forget about his wife's cancer for an hour. But he was not given that choice. The coach jumped straight in to working on Tim's team and Tim went along out of habit.

How Are You?

The purpose of engaging is to reestablish rapport and catch up a bit. Be sure to leave space for the person being coached to share whatever is on his or her mind. We don't want to be mechanical in our conversation. We want to be open, caring, and holistic.

Providing people with an opportunity to begin by talking about whatever they want, people will share about all sorts of things, often bringing closure to what's on their minds, allowing them to fully focus on the rest of the coaching appointment.

Begin the conversation with some variation of the question, "How are you?" Nine times out of ten you'll hear the standard answer, "Fine thank you, and you?" But the question also opens the possibility of sharing any variety of things.

Since beginning coaching conversations by Connecting, I've learned a lot about my coachees. Here are a few of the answers to "How are you?":

- "Great, my daughter won her basketball tournament last night."
- "Terrible, I just got chewed out by my boss for something I didn't do."
- "On the way to the office on my motorcycle, a guy almost ran into me. I laid the bike down. I'm fine, but my knees are still shaking."
- "I've got a bit of a cold."

But most the time, I hear, "I'm fine. How are you?" One question is all it takes to find out.

Connect Example 1:

This dialogue gives an example of a coachee sharing a brief update. The update does not have anything to do with her coaching goals, but it is something she is excited about and wants to share with her coach.

Coach: Hi Susan, how are you?
Coachee: Great.
Coach: What's been happening with you?
Coachee: My son was just accepted at UCLA and received a partial scholarship.
Coach: That is good news!

Coachee: Yeah, we were getting worried since we hadn't heard anything from the university, then on the same day we received the enrollment letter and a scholarship offer. We're all pretty excited.

Coach: I can imagine. Congratulations.

Coachee: Thanks.

Coach: [Pause] Well, are you ready to continue working on your coaching goals?

Coachee: Sure.

Coach: Okay. What progress did you make on your action steps?…

By simply acknowledging Susan's good news she is satisfied and ready to move ahead. The coach directs the conversation towards reviewing action steps and then continues with that day's coaching topic.

Connect Example 2:

It's easy to get caught up in a story about a problem, and jump in to offer coaching help, only to realize at the end of the appointment that the coachee was too polite to stop the conversation and tell you that he or she didn't really need help with that particular issue.

Coach: Hi Dennis, how are you?

Coachee: I'm fine. A bit busy, but what else is new.

Coach: How was your vacation?

Coachee: Oh, we had a good time. It was relaxing to just sit around for a week. Now that I'm back at work, I'm paying for it though.

Coach: How's that?

Coachee: My appointments have been stacked up all week and I've got something like a thousand emails to sort through.

Coach: That's rough…

This dialogue illustrates how a coachee may relate a problem or challenge in his or her life. Don't immediately jump in and begin coaching when you hear a clear problem. In this case, the problem is a busy schedule and a thousand emails.

Don't immediately jump in and begin
coaching when you hear a clear problem.

It is important to clarify whether or not the story (the problem) is simply on the person's mind, or if he or she actually wants help working on it during the coaching conversation. The simplest way is to ask:

(Continued from above)…

Coach: That's rough… [Pause] As we move forward today, what would you like to work on?
Coachee: *I'd like to…* [coachee shares his desired outcome for the conversation]
Coach: Okay, great. Before we dive into that can we take a moment to look back at your action steps?
Coachee: *Sure.*
Coach: What progress did you make?

The coach did not assume that the story Dennis told was the day's coaching topic, instead the coach asked an opened-ended question to discover his agenda for the coaching conversation. The coach then went back to review progress and generate learning from the previous action steps.

Follow-Up Action Steps

The Connect stage of The COACH Model® has two parts. First, engaging with the person you are talking with to build rapport; and secondly, following-up on action steps from the previous coaching conversation. During the first coaching conversation there won't be any action steps to follow-up on. However, each appointment thereafter will build on them. For the purposes of teaching The COACH Model® to those not familiar with it, there is a separate chapter for Follow-Up near the end of the book.

After Connect comes Outcome

After this short relational connection and follow-up of action steps, it is time to move into the current conversation and find out what the coachee wants to work on and what result they would like to achieve by the end of the coaching conversation. By beginning with the end in mind, both the coach and the coachee can move forward with confidence and focus.

Outcome

"Do two walk together unless they have agreed to do so?"
—Amos 3:3

Coaching is an intentional conversation. It is a journey that will result in something meaningful for the person being coached. Rather than a meandering walk without a destination, a coaching conversation usually begins by clarifying where the coachee wants to end up. "Begin with the end in mind,"[7] as Steven Covey wrote. A clear destination, or Outcome, is one of the distinguishing features of coaching and one that makes the conversation intentional.

A clear understanding of the desired outcome near the beginning of the conversation helps in several ways. First, clarifying the outcome of the conversation allows the coachee and coach to be clear on the intended result of the conversation. The coach understands what the coachee wants from the conversation and can partner with the coachee to work toward it.

Second, a clear outcome helps guide the conversation and keep it focused on what the coachee wants to achieve or explore. A conversation without an intended outcome can be directionless—unsure of where it is going and how it is going to get there. Those conversations, more often than not, meander and stray here and there, often ending with little more clarity than when they began. A clear outcome, on the other hand, gives both coach and coachee something specific to work towards, decreasing the chances that the conversation will wander down unneeded rabbit trails.

Third, the results of the conversation can be measured against the intended outcome. As the conversation progresses, it's helpful to check in midway through the conversation and ask the coachee if he or she is satisfied with the progress so far, and whether or not the conversation needs to be adjusted in order to achieve more meaningful results. At the end of the conversation it's easy to know if the conversation has accomplished its purpose by simply comparing what actually happened against the intended outcome.

A clear destination, or Outcome, is one of the distinguishing features of coaching and one that makes the conversation intentional.

Sometimes the value of a coaching conversation is simply to clarify the coachee's problem or goal. Many people feel overwhelmed, and therefore are unable to begin moving forward. The process of clarifying what the coachee wants releases them from these feelings and frees the coachee to move forward towards discovery and action.

Clarity brings hope, which is a powerful motivator. If people aren't clear about their problem or goal, they often won't attempt to work on it because they have no hope for a positive result. Napoleon Bonaparte defined a leader as "a dealer in hope." By clarifying the outcome of coaching conversations, a coach helps instill a sense of hope and confidence in the coachee.

Who Decides the Outcome?

A coachee-driven agenda for the coaching conversation is an important feature in the philosophy of coaching. Adult learning theory tells us that people are more engaged in learning if they have a choice in the topic and can apply it right away.[8] Coaching taps into both these motivations by asking the coachee to choose a topic that is relevant and immediately applicable.

In other helping roles, the helper often assumes the driver's seat in an effort to provide what the other person needs. In coaching, coachees are considered to be the experts on their lives, and are trusted to think, decide, and act. Christian coaches acknowledge the working of the Holy Spirit and trust Him to be guiding and leading the coachee through many different means. Rather than prescribing, advising, or teaching the other person, coaches skillfully help the coachee to reflect more deeply, and draw out how God is guiding them.

The freedom to set one's own agenda for the conversation is a breath of fresh air for many leaders. A pastor wrote me emphasizing this very point. Here's what he had to say:

"What I appreciate most about the coaching I received was that I got to set the agenda. It was very much of a 'me' centered discussion. That may sound somewhat selfish, however in a ministry role where one is always giving, this kind of weekly dialogue was much appreciated. For me, coaching was a relationship where I got to set the agenda and determine what issues needed to be talked about."

What Do You Want?

In the Gospels, there are three separate incidents in which Jesus specifically asks people what they want. Amazing. He has so much to offer, so much insight into their real needs, yet He allowed these people to voice their agenda according to how they perceived their own needs and interests. Let's look at each example.

Two blind men cried out and… "Jesus stopped and called them, 'What do you want me to do for you?' he asked. 'Lord,' they answered, 'we want our sight.' Jesus had compassion on them and touched their eyes. Immediately they received their sight and followed him" (Matthew 20:32-34). The blind men's request and Jesus' response are what we might expect.

In the next case, Andrew and another disciple made a simple and possibly unimportant request. "… Jesus saw them following and asked, 'what do you want?' They said, 'Rabbi' (which means Teacher), 'where are you staying?' 'Come,' he replied, 'and you will see.' So, they went and saw where he was staying, and spent that day with him" (John 1:38-39). It is tempting to think we know what's best for people and to give them something "better" than what they ask for. We might think, "No, what you really need to work on is this…" Jesus didn't brush aside Andrew and Peter's simple request. Instead, he honored it and them by treating as important what they felt was important.

Jesus was always willing to listen to people's requests and desires. But if what they asked for was inappropriate, He did not feel obligated to provide it. James and John's mother's request provides a good example of this. "Then the mother of Zebedee's sons came to Jesus with her sons and, kneeling down, asked a favor of him. 'What is it you want?' he asked. She said, 'Grant that one of these two sons of mine may sit at your right and the other at your left in your kingdom.' 'You don't know what you are asking,' Jesus said to them" (Matthew 20:20-22).

We follow Jesus' example by asking people what they want and allowing them to voice their own concerns and wishes.

Getting on the Same Page

There's a European television commercial that I love.[9] The scene is a city street lined with snow-covered cars. A middle-aged businessperson in a suit and overcoat steps out of a building and begins clearing the snow off of his car. He scrapes and rubs and bangs his hands together to keep warm. Finally, after a lot of hard work, the car is cleared of snow. He steps back with a pleased look on his face and pushes the door unlock button on his remote keychain. "Beep-beep," we hear but nothing happens to his car. As he pushes the button again, the car next to the one he just cleared of snow beeps and its taillights flash as its doors unlock. Slowly it dawns on him that he has cleared snow off of the wrong car.

More times than I'd like to admit, something similar has happened during coaching conversations. As we began the conversation, the coachee mentioned something that sounded like a good coaching topic to me. I began diligently scraping away at the problem to reveal solutions, like the man clearing snow, only at the end to have the coachee say, "Thanks for that. Um, but what I was hoping we could have worked on today was my preparation for our annual meeting… but we're out of time." I coached well, but on the wrong topic!

Through dialogue, the coach and coachee determine
how to best use today's coaching conversation.

It's critical to find out what the coachee considers to be the most valuable topic for that particular coaching conversation. The coach doesn't decide this. Nor does the coach assume that the coaching topic will be a continuation of the previous conversation. The topic may be the next step in a continuing conversation, or it may be something entirely new.

It's the coach's job to draw the topic out of the coachee and then clarify it. Through dialogue, the coach and coachee determine how to best use today's coaching conversation.

Determining the Conversation Outcome

The way you ask the person for their intended outcome communicates something about the conversation you're about to have.

Consider this question: "What would you like to talk about?" If you ask me that question, I have all sorts of things I'd like to talk about: sports, the weather, how to fix my car, a new restaurant I found, etc. But that's not how I want to use our coaching time. Friends talk about whatever is on their minds. But coaching is an intentional conversation that empowers a person to fully live out their calling. Forward movement is not always an important outcome of a friendship conversation.

Contrast that question with this one: "What would you like to work on today?" What do you see emphasized in this question? That's right— working on something. We're not going to *just talk about* something, we are actually going to achieve a helpful result right now. We are beginning with the end in mind. We are creating a destination and purpose for our conversation, all according to what the coachee finds valuable.

Example Outcome Questions:

What would you like to work on?
What would make today's conversation meaningful for you?
What result would you like to take away from our conversation?

Each of the previous questions accomplish several things that are critical to a coaching conversation:

- They put the coachee in the driver's seat in determining the conversation's outcome.
- They assume that there will be a result of some kind.
- They are motivational.

The words "work on," "meaningful," and "result" suggest that there will be progress, which contrasts with the lack of hope that the coachee may have been feeling prior to the conversation.

So, the best way to determine the outcome of the conversation is to simply ask the other person these outcome questions.

Sharpen the Outcome

Asking for the conversation outcome is only the first step in determining the end result of the conversation. Next you need to help the coachee think through what he wants to work on and determine the outcome for the conversation. Through dialogue, the coach and coachee shape the outcome into something that is both useful for the coachee and achievable during the coaching conversation.

Look at the example below to see how the coachee's outcome is brought into sharper focus with a few additional questions.

Coach: "What would you like to work on?"
Coachee: "I want to grow in my relationship with my wife."
Coach: "That's a big topic! What part of this would you like to talk about to move you forward this week?"
Coachee: "I want the relationship we had when we were first married."
Coach: "Could you give a specific example of that kind of relationship?"

Coachee: "Sure. Everything was new and fresh. We had time for each other and it was exciting just to be together. It just doesn't feel like that anymore. It seems like everything we do is focused on the kids or doing work around the house."

Coach: "What makes this important to you right now?"

Coachee: "I feel like we're drifting apart, and don't like it."

Coach: "What does "moving together" rather than "drifting apart" look like?"

Coachee: "We would be together. Not just physically, but mentally present. We'd be growing more internally connected, at a heart level. Right now, we're just dividing up the tasks of running our family."

Coach: "So, what result would you like to take away from our conversation?"

Coachee: "I want time together with my wife that's focused on just us."

Coach: "What specifically would you like to have by the end of our conversation?"

Coachee: "I would like to create a plan to help me regularly connect in heart and mind with my wife."

Coach: "All right."

In this example the coachee gives two general answers: "I want to grow in my relationship with my wife" and "I want the relationship we had when we were first married." It took a few questions to reveal the coachee's actual goal of connecting at a deeper level with his wife. Most likely the coachee wasn't fully aware that connecting with his wife in heart and mind was his real need. Already, the coaching process produced additional clarity for the coachee. If the coach had not continued clarifying the desired outcome, the conversation may have moved to any number of more shallow aspects of his marriage rather than the result he actually desired.

Use questions to explore, clarify, and focus the coachee's topic, problem, or goal. As the coachee defines his intended results through a dialogue, he increases his own awareness and gains clarity on the issue even before thoroughly discussing the topic. Just defining an outcome is often a welcome relief for an overwhelmed coachee.

Just defining an outcome is often a
welcome relief for an overwhelmed coachee.

Exploring Questions

Exploring questions examine the topic that the coachee wants to work on in order to understand it more fully. Don't be afraid to dig below the surface.

Many times, coachees give a "how-to" topic, like time-management, controlling email, or some other task. While this issue may be real and pressing, it may be more helpful to move quickly from the surface "how-to" issue to a deeper "being" discussion. Explore the topic with questions like,

- If you could accomplish that, what would it do for you?
- What's going on *in* you that is keeping you from doing this?

Once the coachee can sort out what's happening inside them, they often can quickly address the "how-to" part of the solution.

It's also not uncommon for a coachee to suggest a topic that is actually a solution to a larger problem or goal. By understanding what's behind the specific topic, the coach can understand the coachee's motivations, reasoning, and assumptions. All three of these points are worth exploring. Sometimes when looking beyond the narrow topic, coaches are able to help the coachee identify other ways to achieve their ultimate aim. Discovering and working directly on the coachee's ultimate goal saves the coachee time and effort.

Look at the following example:

Coach: What result would you like to take away from our conversation?

Coachee: I need a plan to save $100,000.

Coach: What is the $100,000 for?

Coachee: To pay for an MBA program I want to join.

Coach: Oh, you want to join an MBA program? What would an MBA do for you?

Coachee: I'd be able to quit my current job and make more money.

Coach: Ultimately, your goal is to change jobs and make more money.

Coachee: Yes, that's right. I feel like I'm going nowhere in my current job and want to get out.

Coach: An MBA might help you find a better job, it also requires a lot of time and money. Would you be open to exploring other options to find a new job?

Coachee: Sure.

With a few questions, the coach uncovered the coachee's reasoning, motivations, and ultimate goal for needing $100,000. It's possible that the best way for the coachee to change jobs and make more money is indeed to get an MBA. At the same time, there are many other approaches to this goal that do not require $100,000 and two years of study. Either way, by exploring what's behind the topic of saving $100,000, both the coach and coachee were able to clarify the real purposes, and thus can approach the topic in a more holistic way.

Example Exploring Questions:

Let's back up a minute, what are some of the issues behind this situation?

What's the big picture here, what do you want to achieve?
What would achieving this do for you?

The question "What would achieving this do for you?" is especially helpful in uncovering and understanding a person's motivations for doing something. All goals have a number of motivations behind them. People tend to reveal *what* they want, not *what motivates* them to want it, which is often what they really desire in the first place. Clarifying motivations often reveal the coachee's ultimate goal and is a powerful tool to use in helping the coachee to move forward.

Clarifying Questions

We all make assumptions about the meaning of words or phrases. Sometimes our assumptions are correct and other times they are not. It's best to ask. After asking, you may find out that you both held the same understanding for the word or phrase. Still, you could ask about the motivations behind it. Such as in this dialogue:

Coach: What would you like to work on today?
Coachee: I'd like to figure out how our team can become a real team.
Coach: What does a "real team" mean to you?
Coachee: We would have a common goal with each of us playing a role in accomplishing it, and we'd get something done.
Coach: What makes becoming a real team meaningful to you?
Coachee: I want to achieve something bigger than just what I personally can do on my own. And I want to work together with

others. Right now, we call ourselves a team, but we're each working on our own things.

Coach: So, you're looking for a big, common goal and teamwork in accomplishing it?

Coachee: Yes, that's right.

Coach: What part of this would you like to work on today?

[The dialogue continues to further explore the topic and create a specific outcome for the conversation.]

Clarifying questions allow you to explore what the coachee means by the words they are using. Clarifying questions are not just for your understanding, but also to promote greater clarity in the coachee. Clarification usually produces a more straightforward and clear explanation. Pick up on vague or possibly meaningful words or phrases the coachee uses and ask for clarification.

Example Clarifying Questions:

What do you mean by "act like a team"?
What's an example of "community"?
What would being "successful" look like to you?

Focusing Questions

Focusing questions help to narrow the coaching topic to something that is both manageable to achieve during the length of the conversation, and immediately helpful to the coachee. It's not unusual for coachees to suggest a broad or vague topic.

Don't worry. There are simple ways to narrow the topic to something manageable. Look at how this example works:

Coach: What would you like to focus on today?

Coachee: I'd like to achieve world peace.

Coach: That's an important topic. What part of that would you like to work on today?

Coachee: I'd like to see Christians and Muslims get along better.

Coach: Ah. And what aspect of this relationship would be immediately helpful to you this week?

Coachee: There's a new Muslim center opening a few blocks away from my home and I'm embarrassed by my neighbor's reactions. I'd like to think through some positive responses.

[The conversation may continue to further clarify the topic.]

Of course, this is an exaggerated example, but it serves to illustrate a few points. First, the coach didn't panic. She affirmed the topic as important and asked a question to narrow it further. Second, the coach didn't assume that she understood the topic. World peace is a huge topic that includes many things. Any guess by the coach would likely be wrong. Asking the coachee to explain what he or she means is the only way to ensure that you have a complete understanding of their thought process. Third, the coach didn't dismiss the topic. Some might have responded to the coachee's desire for world peace by asking, "How about we work on something more practical?" Instead, she engaged the coachee's topic and found that there was a practical situation behind it. Fourth, the coach didn't narrow the topic herself. Broad, vague topics can be intimidating.

For many people, a natural response to a topic viewed as "unrealistic" would be to gain control of the conversation by being directive and offering the coachee a couple of topics related to world peace to discuss. It's much better to ask focusing questions to the help the coachee self-reflect on what's important to them.

Example Focusing Questions:

That's a big topic, what part of that would you like to focus on today?

What aspect of that problem would you like to work on right now?

What part of this topic would be most helpful for you to address this week?

Again, don't be tempted to assume you understand what the coachee would like to work on or to narrow the topic for the coachee. Instead, use clarifying questions to help the coachee separate the broad topic into smaller topics, and to prioritize what today's conversation will be about.

Use clarifying questions to help the coachee
prioritize what today's conversation will be about.

Confirm the Outcome

As the outcome becomes more specific and clearer, test your understanding by asking the coachee to restate his or her outcome. Or you can summarize the outcome yourself. Be careful not to go beyond what the coachee has said by adding meaning or specifics the coachee didn't mention.

Just so we're clear, would you please restate what you'd like to achieve today?

Is that what you'd like to focus our conversation on today?

Today, you'd like to leave with X, Y, and Z. Is that correct?

Checking Progress During the Conversation

Asking for the coachee's desired outcome and then using exploring, clarifying, and focusing questions to sharpen the topic will ensure that you are working on what is most important and meaningful for the coachee.

At any time during the conversation you can check on progress by referring back to the outcome. Ask something like this, "How are we doing at getting to what you hoped for in our conversation?" This check-in allows the coachee to express what progress they feel they've made so far in the conversation and what still needs to be discussed.

It's not unusual for the coachee to have thoughts about the coaching topic that haven't been expressed yet, because the conversation didn't flow there. Asking the above question, along with "What would you like to explore next?" gives the coachee the control of the conversation. Remember, coaching is about helping the coachee explore and learn, not the coach figuring things out and leading the coachee to their answer.

With a clear outcome, the conversation can move toward exploring the topic in order to raise awareness and additional perspective. During this exploration you might travel down several different paths. Having a clear outcome in place allows both you and the coachee to more easily determine whether the conversation is moving in the right direction.

Awareness

*"I pray also that the eyes of your heart may be enlightened
in order that you may know the hope to which he has called
you, the riches of his glorious inheritance in the saints, and
his incomparably great power for us who believe."*
—Ephesians 1:18-19a

Discoveries—insights both large and small—are a fundamental part of the coaching experience and are the ultimate goal of the Awareness step. Coachees make discoveries about themselves, their situation, their potential, their actions, their inaction, their assumptions, their values—the list goes on and on. The thrill of discovery produces new thoughts, emotions, perspectives, and determination.

Coaches facilitate these discoveries and help coachees take action based on their insights. As their perspective expands and their current situation becomes clearer, coachees see more options for action and change. The greater the discovery, the more readily options for action will present themselves. In this chapter you will learn the skill of creating powerful questions that enable others to reflect more deeply than they might on their own. You will learn how to ask questions that will raise awareness from many different perspectives, and you will learn how to stimulate insights by generating feedback rather than giving it.

New Roads, New Perspective

Once, while I was traveling in France for a speaking engagement, I set my GPS for a small city in the south, half the country away from my starting point just outside of Paris. The GPS directed me along a small two-lane road that took me through fields and cute country villages.

As beautiful as it was, the journey was taking longer than I expected. Every 15 minutes or so I became stuck behind a slow-moving tractor. I tried everything I could to improve my speed on this road. I passed the tractors and anything else that was in front of me. On straight sections of road, I increased my speed. I didn't stop for anything. This continued for two hours. According to my GPS, it would still take three *more* hours to reach my destination. I was going to be very late. But what could I do?

Since I was going to be late anyway and still had a long way to go, I decided to stop for an espresso and a croissant. After this heavenly refreshment, I turned on the car again and the GPS reset itself. Only then did I realize that the GPS had been previously set to "avoid toll roads." After I changed the GPS settings to *include* toll roads, it mapped out a new route and gave me a fresh arrival time of only 58 minutes. That's two hours faster than the route I had been using.

"Do you have eyes but fail to see, and ears but fail to hear?"
—Jesus, Mark 8:18

Our thinking is like a road we travel on. We explore, reflect, act, and adjust our actions—all along our line of thinking. After we've explored all that we can, if we get stuck, we find someone to help us. We explain the situation to them, using our line of thinking. More often than not, the person helping will also follow our line of thinking—the road we present to them. They help us explore it further, but it's already tapped out. Their help may produce one or two further steps of incremental progress, but we're still traveling along the same old road.

Breakthrough comes when we find new roads altogether, rather than traveling more quickly and overcoming obstacles on old roads. The struggles of the old road often become irrelevant when we discover a new road. Just as on the toll roads in France, I had no further need to find solutions to slow-moving tractors and small villages.

How do we find new roads? Usually not in the places we've been taught to look.

Information ≠ Answers

It is commonly believed that the key to finding answers and getting unstuck is through more information or knowledge. So, we seek experts through books, seminars, podcasts, and blogs, hoping they will give us that new little tidbit of knowledge—the key to solving our problem.

Breakthrough, however, rarely comes through new knowledge, because looking at additional information from the same perspective just keeps us on the same road.

Coaching takes a different approach. The focus is not on new information or knowledge, but rather on a new perspective. A shift in perspective—seeing what we already "know" with new eyes—can lead to the discovery of new roads. A narrow perspective tends to limit thinking. The more perspective, the more accurately a person will see his or her situation.

We find new roads by increasing our perspective—seeing the same world in new ways, through new eyes. With a new perspective we make discoveries about our situation and ourselves. Insights come through pursuing these new lines of thinking. As a result, we are immediately presented with new options for action that are significantly different from before. We move from being stuck and "having tried everything," to seeing many new possibilities and feeling hope once again for success.

"The real voyage of discovery consists not in seeking new landscapes but in having new eyes."
—Marcel Proust

Once we see with new eyes and gain increased perspective we're more likely to discover breakthrough solutions.

Why Knowledge is a Thing of the Past

As leaders, we often view ourselves as knowledge providers. So, we teach, tell, or advise and, in this way, pass on our knowledge to someone else. The instruction process requires the other person to listen as we share our knowledge. The assumption is that what we have to say will be the key to solving the other person's problem or will help them achieve their goal.

This is sometimes helpful, but knowledge, even the knowledge that worked for us in the past, isn't as powerful as generating insight in the other person. We own what we discover.

Don't get me wrong, I love studying what's already been said and done on a topic. That information is invaluable. However, it is only one type of learning. I believe there is deeper learning that goes beyond existing knowledge and how others have applied that knowledge. Deeper learning actually creates new ideas, applications, and actions that neither the coach nor the coachee were aware of before.

Creating something new requires engaged and reflective thinking. This is where powerful questions come in. Asking the right questions promotes reflection more effectively than merely providing knowledge. Coaches use questions as a primary tool in working with others. Questions help stimulate thinking, broaden perspective, and generate new options for actions.

Let's look at the difference between knowledge and questions:

Knowledge is past;
Questions are future.

Knowledge is static;
Questions are dynamic.

Knowledge is rigid;
Questions are flexible.

Knowledge limits options;
Questions create possibilities.

Knowledge requires adaptation;
Questions call for innovation.

Knowledge is a location;
Questions are a journey.

Knowledge can be superior;
Questions require humility.

Knowledge knows;
Questions learn.

Powerful Questions for Perspective

Powerful questions are the tools that help coachees to discover new roads and to find answers. Many people are not naturally reflective, and we all have a limited perspective. Coaches stimulate or even *provoke* reflection with questions that cause coachees to think more deeply than they would on their own.

But why ask questions? Isn't it faster to just tell people your ideas and share your experience? Why not just give people the answer?

Lyle Schaller is a name you may not be familiar with, yet he did for church and denominational consulting what Peter Drucker did for corporations. In fact, the two men were friends. Schaller focused on bringing change to organizations and believed in the power of questions. He wrote, "The most effective way to influence both individual and institutional behavior is to ask questions."[10] This powerful statement goes against the grain of common leadership practices. Many of us act as if instructing, reminding, inspiring, preaching, convincing, commanding, or announcing will change the behavior of others. Schaller's years of consulting experience in more than 60 denominations provided him with ample opportunity to try all these "telling" approaches, but he settled on questions as the most effective method. "Change is the name of the game," he wrote, "and questions are the heart of that game!"[11]

Coaches stimulate or even *provoke* reflection with questions that cause coachees to think more deeply than they would on their own.

How do questions promote change? According to adult educator Jane Vella, "Open questions are the single sure practice that invites critical thinking and effective learning."[12] Adults learn best through dialogue, and questions promote dialogue. Critical or analytical thinking is an open, non-defensive examination of a topic. As Vella found, reflection is best accomplished through dialogue. To dialogue is to hold a topic in front of you and examine it from different sides. Open questions allow the topic to be viewed in new ways, producing new discoveries and thus, learning.

How To Ask Powerful Questions

One of the most frequently asked questions at our coaching workshops is, "How do I ask powerful questions?" It would be nice if there were a list of pre-formed, set questions that were guaranteed to unlock perspective and insights in others. Unfortunately, there are few "magic" questions. Powerful questions are not that easy to come by!

"The purposes of a person's heart are deep waters,
but one who has insight draws them out."
—Proverbs 20:5

Powerful questions come from profound *listening* and *engagement* with a person. What makes a question powerful is its ability to provoke reflection in the other person. Many of us are used to telling people about our own reflections rather than drawing out theirs. To ask powerful questions, it's helpful to keep three principles in mind.

1. Coachee or Me?
   Is this question for my benefit or the coachee's?

2. Forward or Backward?

    Is this question focused on the past or moving forward?

3. Building or Correcting?

    Does this question try to correct the coachee or help them build?

Coachee or Me?

Powerful questions are for the benefit of the other person. Not the asker. Questions are based on the other person's agenda, not the coach's. We saw in the last chapter that the Outcome of the conversation will come from the coachee, but it's possible that the coach can hijack the agenda during the Awareness stage.

One way a coach might do this is by asking questions for their own benefit, instead of the coachee's. This problem stems from the mindset of the coach. If the coach views himself or herself as a solution provider, then they must know all the details of the situation in order to give a helpful solution.

For example, if the topic is a conflict, a solution-provider coach will need to hear all the details in order to offer advice on how the coachee might solve the conflict. Who knows those details? The coachee. Who doesn't? The coach. However, if the coach views himself or herself as someone who helps the coachee reflect to find their own solutions, the coach needs to know very few details of the conflict. The coach focuses on the Process of solving the conflict by asking powerful questions.

> **Coach-focused question: Tell me about the conflict.** (The coachee knows about the conflict, thus the question is for the coach.)
> **Coachee-focused question: What would excellent resolution of this conflict look like?**

Forward or Backward?

Powerful questions are forward-moving not backward-looking. This principle builds on the first, if the coach isn't providing solutions, then she needs to know very little of the background. The coachee already knows the background information. Other helping styles may spend the bulk of the conversation discussing all the details and background information. That history may be interesting, but this practice often does little to further the goal of new insights and perspectives.

One of the key differences between therapy and coaching is that a counselor or therapist seeks to discover issues in a person's past that are preventing them from moving forward in their life. Special techniques and tools are used to understand these issues in order to bring healing or closure. While both counselors and coaches use many of the same dialogue techniques, coaching begins in the present and is future oriented. Coachees are basically psychologically and emotionally healthy and want to move ahead. If you suspect a coachee has a psychological disorder such as depression, addictions, eating disorders, or suicidal tendencies, coach the person to find a qualified counselor or therapist so he or she can get the help they need.

This is not to say that a coach never asks questions regarding the past. Sometimes helping a coachee link their previous experience to their current situation produces insight. The point is, you need to know far fewer details of the coachee's situation than you might think you do, so focus on asking questions that are forward-looking.

> **Backward-looking question: Why did you organize it that way?** (The coach wants the history, but it may not be needed.)
> **Forward-looking question: What approach is your intuition telling you to take?**

Building or Correcting?

Powerful questions stimulate discovery toward action and do not subtly attempt to correct the coachee. No matter how impartial you try to be, you will still make mental judgments about the coachee's situation. These judgments can leak through in the form of questions that you hope will help the coachee realize their errors. These kinds of questions are intended to "raise awareness" and correct the coachee.

There are a couple of problems with this approach. We can easily break trust with the coachee if they sense that we are judging them. The coachee's natural reaction is to close up, become defensive, and justify their actions. The coachee can also feel manipulated. They view your questions as an attempt to "fix" them rather than as honest inquiry. Also, some coachees may believe that you actually have the answer for them and that you are holding back. This does not promote trust or self-discovery.

People want help, but they don't want to be fixed.

Don't focus your questions on correcting the coachee, but rather on ways that will allow the coachee to build. Throughout a coaching conversation the coachee builds understanding, perspective, options, solutions, and actions.

> **Correcting question: Why haven't you delegated this to someone else?** (Coach is thinking, "You should have delegated this a long time ago.")
> **Building question: What help do you need from here?** (Just using the word "delegation" provides a suggestion, if not a

judgment. Leave it open with "help" and see what ideas come to the coachee.)

Moving From Your Ideas to Theirs

We all have ideas. There's a saying, "Ideas are like small children. Other people's are nice, but we always like our own the best." This holds true with coaches too. We like our ideas. They make sense to us, and we think they will be helpful to the coachee.

So, what do we do with the ideas that pop into our head during the coaching conversation? Let's look at how ideas are often shared.

- If I were you I'd ask Susan to help.
- You should ask Susan to help you.
- If you were smart, you'd ask Susan to help you.
- Susan is quite capable, how about asking her to help you?

These examples of sharing an idea have plenty of downsides to them. "If I were you...," the coachee may be thinking, "well, you are not me." "You should..." or "ought to" or "if you were smart you would..." are all commands and place judgment on the other person if they don't respond positively to our idea. The last of the four examples above offers at least a bit of reasoning and considers the coachee's opinion. However, the biggest problem with these suggestions is that they are the coach's ideas, and do not draw from the coachee's own resources.

"Transformation comes more from pursuing
profound questions than seeking practical answers."
—Peter Block[13]

In some helping roles, sharing your ideas with the other person is considered a normal function. However, a coaching approach draws out ideas from the coachee and their surrounding resources, helping them reflect on the merits and application of these ideas. The generation of ideas from within the coachee is a key approach.

The purpose of providing an idea is to help the coachee find a solution. When we provide a solution, we short-circuit the reflective process that equips the coachee to find his or her own solutions. According to the old parable, we mistakenly give them a fish rather than teaching them to fish.

My-Idea Questions

Even as we use questions, we may still be sharing our ideas. Take a look at these questions:

- Are you planning to borrow money to do that?
- Could Susan help you?
- How about asking for a new computer?
- Do you learn from reading books or talking with people?

I call this type of question a my-idea question. My-idea questions are a vehicle for our own ideas or suggestions. This type of question is the easiest to ask because it is basically giving advice in the form of a question. My-idea questions flow directly from our own perspective toward the solutions or the next steps that we see.

My-idea questions limit the coachee's reflection because the coachee must answer yes or no to the coach's idea. In the case of "or" questions, there are two ideas the coachee can choose from—but both are from the coach. Powerful questions are those that provoke reflection in the other person. My-idea questions do not generate this type of creative, deep reflection.

An alternative is to ask open questions. The response to an open question can go in a hundred different directions. Asking open questions requires the coach to give up control of the conversation and be willing to go where the Holy Spirit and the coachee leads. That lack of control can be scary for a coach.

Opening Up Questions

Your ideas are not going to go away, so use them. Instead of forming your ideas into my-idea questions, use them to create open questions. Asking open questions will help you move from being an idea-giver to an idea-explorer.

The technique of creating open questions involves taking your idea and broadening it to its root topic or category. By asking about the broader category, you encourage the coachee to reflect and find their own answer. Here's how you can do this.

For most people a specific idea, suggestion or direction will pop into their head. If you directly create a question with your idea it will be a my-idea question. Here's an example. During a conversation about purchasing some land for a ministry the coach asks, "Are you planning to borrow money to do that?" How many options are there? One. Whose idea is it to borrow money? The coach's. The coach is using a my-idea question to give an idea, suggestion, or basically an answer disguised as a question. "Borrow money" is too specific an idea to provoke reflection in the coachee.

Instead, take your idea and broaden it to the wider category or topic that it is a part of and ask about that. In this example the idea is to "borrow money." So, back the idea up and broaden it to the category or topic that it is a part of. The category or topic behind the idea of "borrow money" is really how to *pay for it*, so you might ask, "What are your plans to pay for that?" How many options does this question present? Many. Who provides the options? The coachee. This is an open question.

Let's try another example. Rather than asking, "Could Susan help you?" Ask, "Who could help you?" Immediately the coachee goes from one possibility (Susan) to a multitude of possibilities (anyone). Here are more examples.

My-idea question: I have a helpful book on managing teams, would you like to read it?
Open question: How could you learn more about managing teams?

My-idea question: Have you thought about firing him?
Open question: What options do you see in working with him?

My-idea question: Is casting vision the next step for the team?
Open question: What are possible next steps for the team?

My-idea question: Could someone on your team help?
Open question: Who might be able to help?

My-idea question: Do you learn from reading books or talking with people?
Open question: How do you prefer to learn new things?

Both my-idea questions and open questions follow a pattern. Typically, my-idea questions begin with the words would, could, are, is, and does, while open questions begin with what or how. Table 2 lists typical starting words for both types of questions.

Asking Questions from Different Angles
One sure way to help people discover new roads and increase perspective is by asking questions from different angles. Angles are the perspectives,

TYPICAL MY-IDEA AND OPEN QUESTION WORDS	
My-Idea Questions	**Open Questions**
• Would...	• What...
• Could...	• How...
• Are...	• Who...
• Is...	• Where...
• Does...	• When...
• Have you thought of...	• In what ways...

Table 3

or the roads our thinking travels along. If our thinking stays on the same road, solutions will be limited to those that are available on that road. However, there are many roads—many ways to think about something—and just as many perspectives.

When the coachee presents their situation to us it's natural that we will see it immediately from two perspectives, our own and the coachee's. It's easy to get stuck on *either* road—either perspective. Instead, the coach can ask questions from different perspectives, or what we call angles. Angles are similar to the topic or categories we used above in open questions. Common angles to explore are: relational, financial, motivational, organizational, spiritual, etc.

Here's an example. Jennifer was country director for a large humanitarian organization. She shared with me about a conflict with another field leader. She described the conflict as a personal attack by the other leader. She told me that she'd never gotten along with the other leader and found him to be arrogant and self-serving. As we explored the coachee's perspective, we couldn't find any leverage for action. She was stuck and unable to move forward.

Then we looked at the conflict from the angle of organizational culture.

I asked, "How might organizational culture be affecting your relationship?"

"I don't see any link because our organization is empowering, very decentralized and flat in its structure," she said.

"How does an empowered, decentralized leader behave?" I probed.

"Independently." She answered.

"And how is your colleague behaving?" I continued.

"Independently… we all do. But I'm trying to work together, and he said he wanted to as well. This is one thing that is so tough in my organization—nobody works together."

"So, you're saying it's rare that leaders in your organization partner between fields?"

"Yes."

"So, how might that aspect of your corporate culture be adding to your conflict with this field leader?"

"Actually, he's not behaving much differently than everyone else, I just expected that we'd be able to partner together, and he indicated that he'd like to partner as well. But our organization doesn't have a good history of that kind of partnership."

"Keep going."

"Well, I'm seeing that it's more than just him and me here. We are trying to swim upstream in our organizational culture. I had high expectations, maybe unrealistic, and possibly he did as well."

"With the corporate culture in mind, how might you think differently about this field leader and your expectations of partnership?"

"I still expect him to keep his word. But I also realize that we have our organizational history going against us. I shouldn't take his lack of action so personally. Actions that I see as self-serving and arrogant could be interpreted as him just doing his own thing, like everyone does. There's a big difference between a good idea or something we 'should' do and something strategic enough for us to overcome our personal habits and organizational culture."

"Those are helpful insights."

Changing angles again, I asked, "If you think about his personality and yours, how might personality differences be affecting your partnership?"

Asking questions from different angles allows the coachee to reflect on their situation from different perspectives. I use angle questions quite freely. Sometimes I have a hunch that there might be something to be gained from exploring a certain angle. Other times, I simply ask an angle question to see what new reflection it may provoke. The goal is to raise awareness and increase the perspective of the coachee.

Asking questions from different angles allows the coachee to reflect on their situation from different perspectives.

If you ask an angle questions that falls flat, that is, the coachee sees no relevance, then just move on. The key is to get the coachee off of the road they have been traveling on—their own perspective—and help them explore different roads. Some roads are dead-ends. You will need to turn around and head in another direction. Other roads are like expressway on-ramps that quickly take the coachee's thinking to new places.

25 Angles

Angles are different perspectives from which to discuss a situation. Any topic, category, or perspective could be formed into an Angle question. Here are 25 examples:

1. Relational: What are the relational dynamics?
2. Background: Step back for a moment, what are the underlying issues?
3. Spiritual: From a spiritual perspective what do you see?
4. Culture: How might culture play a part in this situation?
5. Personality: How might personality (yours or others') be influencing things?
6. Financial: If money weren't an issue, how would that change things?
7. Emotion: What role are emotions playing in this situation?
8. Intuition: What is your gut telling you?
9. Information: What additional information do you need?
10. People: Who might be able to give you a different perspective?
11. Organizational: How might your organizational structure be influencing things?
12. Environment: What things around you are holding you back?
13. Community: In what ways is your community impacting you?
14. Values: Which of your values are you trying to honor in this situation?
15. Calling: What parts of this connects to your calling?
16. Spouse: What does your spouse think about this?
17. Family: How is your family being affected in this situation?
18. Employer: Where does your boss fit in?
19. Experience: How have you handled this in the past?
20. Priority: How important is this to you?
21. Motivation: What would overcoming this situation do for you personally?
22. Loss: What do you have to give up to move forward?
23. Time: What difference would it make if you had 3 days/months/years?

24. Energy: Which parts of this give you energy?
25. Jesus: What would Jesus do?[14]

Awareness Through Feedback

Another way to raise awareness is to provide feedback. The goal of feedback is for the coachee to have useful information to help them improve and develop. This information can reinforce positive behaviors or identify blind spots. Feedback is both reinforcing and corrective in nature.

However, all feedback is not received the same way. There's a world of difference between "positive" feedback—acknowledgment and encouragement—and corrective feedback. Let's face it *nobody* likes to hear critical feedback.

The biggest obstacle in giving corrective feedback is breaking through the person's defenses so that they will be able to somewhat objectively evaluate what is shared with them.

We often use tricks to make feedback more palatable, like the "feedback sandwich" in which you give a critical feedback sandwiched between two affirming comments. Or the 3 + 1 feedback where you give three positive points first to warm them up to the one corrective feedback. I have a friend who told me about his experience on the receiving end of this approach. The conversation went like this:

"Becky, nice job keeping the group discussion on track today," her colleague Paul started.

"Thanks," she replied, feeling genuinely affirmed.

"And I noticed how you drew out the quiet people," Paul continued. In Becky's mind defensive alarm bells start humming softly. "He just gave me two complements in a row," she thought, "If there's a third I'm in trouble."

Paul went on, "Also, I appreciate how you pushed us to action steps." Three. She knew it! Something negative is coming next. She could feel her heart beating faster and heat in her face. In her mind, she already began discounting what he might say—even before she heard it. "Funny," she told me, "I didn't feel defensive at all after the first complement."

Her colleague continued, "I wonder if I could give you some feedback..."

"Sure," she replied. We have to say this, don't we?

"It's been nearly a year now, and you still lead every section of the meeting. Others, like Jeremy, are quite capable and would feel empowered if you were to call on them to lead different sections."

"Jeremy?" Becky thought, "Why are you always promoting Jeremy? And anyway, meetings used to be a waste of time until I took over and started leading them. Now we get things done. I'm not willing to sacrifice that just so your buddy Jeremy can have his moment in the spotlight."

But what she said was, "Thanks, I'll consider that."

Just about everyone feels defensive when faced with critical feedback—some are just better at hiding it! So, how can we give feedback that people will hear? The answer is simple. Don't give it.

Raise Awareness by Not Giving Feedback

Sir John Whitmore, a British former race-car driver who later coached executives and professional athletes, took a different view on where feedback should originate. He wrote, "Generating high-quality relevant feedback, as far as possible from within rather than from experts, is essential for continuous improvement, at work, in sport and in all aspects of life."[15]

"Generating" is not the term we usually use to describe the feedback process. We "give" feedback, which often triggers defensiveness. Whitmore suggests we generate feedback from within the coachee rather than from experts—you or anyone else. How do we generate feedback from within the coachee? Through powerful questions!

You can generate feedback from within the coachee using a simple three-step process.

1. What did you do well?
    Ask about what the coachee did well. Explore these behaviors and the results. Reinforce these positive behaviors.
2. What could you improve?
    Ask the coachee in what way they think they could improve. Talk about what that improvement might be and what results they would expect to see.
3. How would you do it differently next time?
    Generate some possible future alternatives. Coach through how the coachee will do it next time.

Generate feedback by asking questions to
avoid defensiveness and increase buy-in.

Let's consider how things might have been different if Paul had generated feedback in Becky, rather than giving it. Using the three step process for generating feedback, let's imagine how Paul might have guided Becky through self-reflection on how she led the meeting and how she could improve in the future.

"Becky, good meeting today." Paul started.

"Thanks." Becky replied.

"Would it be helpful to debrief it for a minute?" Paul offered.

"Sure."

"What do you think you did well?"

"I kept the group discussion on track."

"I noticed that too. Good job. What else?"

"We got to action steps today, which is an improvement."

"How did you do that?"

"I kept pushing for people to be specific and to commit to what, who, and when."

"Yes, those gentle encouragements, along with not continuing the discussion without action steps, made a big difference."

"Thanks."

"What could you improve?"

"My goal this last meeting was to make sure action steps got nailed down…"

"You did that well."

"I was thinking that I'd like to involve others in running the meetings."

"What do you mean?"

"Well, right now I do all the planning and upfront facilitation. I'd like to see others do part of that."

"How might you do that next time?"

"Maybe Darlene could facilitate the discussion in some creative way. She's good at that. There are two topics we need to work on next week. I could outline the topics and Darlene could lead a discussion to generate some options."

"Sounds good. Will you do that next week?"

"Yes, I'll talk with Darlene later today about it."

"Okay. Well, once again, nice work on how you led the meeting. I thought it was very productive."

Finding New Roads

We began this chapter by exploring how our line of thinking is like a road. Not every road will get us to where we want to go. All too often we stay on our comfortable roads. Through coaching conversations, you can help people gain perspective, find new roads, make discoveries, and find their own ideas.

Asking open questions, rather than my-idea questions gives the coachee freedom to explore without the limitations of the coach's ideas. Questions from different angles take exploration in new directions. Each angle is like a new road lined with discoveries and perspective. Finally, by generating rather than giving feedback we can help a person to reflect more deeply on their actions, without the defensiveness that often accompanies outside feedback.

With new roads, discoveries, and increased perspective come new options for action. Gone is the slow progress of the old road. In its place are new roads with all sorts of possibilities for new actions. And action and application are the direction that the coaching conversation moves to next.

Course

*"You see that his faith and his actions were working together,
and his faith was made complete by what he did."*
—James 2:22

"Plans fail for lack of counsel, ..." wrote the wise man (Proverbs 15:22). What was true 3,000 years ago is still true today. Yet there are many ways to counsel. Coaches help people to generate multiple options and understand more clearly the possible outcome and consequences of each option available to them. This process helps move the coachee to action.

Reflection and discussion are not ends in themselves. Reflection must move beyond warm thoughts and clever insights to application. Action steps put feet to insights and discoveries. Helping people move into action is one of the key roles of a coach. Without action steps, discoveries and insights are just good ideas.

Coaching to create action steps is relatively easy if the Awareness stage was done well. Ideas for action naturally flow from new perspectives and awareness. Coaches help people create action steps using the conversational skills of active listening and powerful questions. The coach is responsible for the process of generating action steps, but not for giving action steps or "homework" to the coachee.

Coaching helps coachees to create action steps that will move them forward toward their goal. While each action step is 100% up to the coachee to decide, through dialogue the coach asks clarifying questions regarding what the action step will look like, how it will be done, and realistic timing. Good coaching balances ambition (or lack of it) and practical planning, resulting in greater forward movement.

Helping people move into action is one of the key roles of a coach.

After the Reflection...

If you boil a pot of seawater until the water completely evaporates, you will be left with salt. If we boil the practice of coaching down to its core elements, we find reflection and application. Reflection will guide the coachee to important insights, and these insights will lead to application in the form of action steps. These core elements follow the Action-Reflection Cycle.

Coaches use active listening and powerful questions to help people explore their own hearts and reflect on their situations. This process produces insight, expanded perspective, and new "ah-ha" or "oh-no" moments. These moments are thrilling as clouds of confusion lift and relief streams in like the sun, giving the coachee new hope. For that hope to be realized, the person must take his or her insights and put them into practice—and that can be hard work.

Remaining in the intangible world of theory and ideas can sometimes feel safer. It can feel cozy to wrap ourselves in the spiritual mystery of reflection and insights. To act on insights requires that we come down from the mountaintop of reflection and risk applying our insights and ideas in the real world.

It's easy to stop and be satisfied with a new insight or change in perspective. Good thoughts followed by a lack of action are nothing new. The Lord criticized Israel for the same thing, "My people come to you, as they usually do, and sit before you to listen to your words, but they do not put them into practice" (Ezekiel 33:31). It is easier to just keep doing what we have been doing, rather than doing the things necessary to change.

The tension between reflection and action is an age-old problem, to which the Bible also speaks. The book of James portrays faith—our beliefs, ideals, and values—as being at odds with *acting* on our faith. James argues the case for faith in action in James 2:14-26:

- "...faith by itself, if it is not accompanied by action is dead."
- "...I will show you my faith by what I do."
- "You see that his faith and his actions were working together and his faith was made complete by what he did."

Faith and action—insights and action steps—are not mutually exclusive. The relationship is symbiotic. Insights produce actions. Actions complete insights. Faith not acted upon is only potential faith, which, according to James, is dead.

> "We don't think ourselves into a new way of acting,
> we act ourselves into a new way of thinking."
> —Bossidy, Charan & Burck in *Execution*.

Jesus encouraged His followers to apply His teaching; "Therefore everyone who hears these words of mine and puts them into practice is like a wise man who built his house on the rock" (Matthew 7:24). So did the Apostle Paul when he wrote, "Whatever you have learned or received or heard from me, or seen in me—put it into practice" (Philippians 4:9).

The Source of Actions Steps

Few Christians question the role of the Holy Spirit in providing insights through the reflection process. The same Holy Spirit is also the source of action steps. Look at Philippians 2:13, "…for it is God who works in you to will and to act according to his good purpose." God will give people the will (desire and motivation) and the ability to act. He is the source of action steps—those actions that complete the insights He provided during reflection.

Action steps are a powerful way in which people live out their calling. We use the same spiritual discovery process as in the Awareness Stage to generate Spirit-willed action steps for the purpose of living out those insights. Insights without action steps are only half formed. God's desire for us is to complete Spirit-directed insights by putting them into action.

> God's desire for us is to complete Spirit-
> directed insights by putting them into action.

The Anatomy Of An Action Step

Action steps are the transitions from thoughts and insights to action and application. In the remainder of this chapter I will show you how to help coachees create action steps that will give them the best chance of success.

Not all action steps are created equal. Some actions steps are doomed to fail from the beginning. The action step may be too big, irrelevant, or the coachee may have no idea how to actually accomplish it.

Action steps are not always physical actions. Sometimes actions steps entail further reflection on the topic at hand. Consulting with someone and asking their opinion is an action step. Researching a topic is an action step. Reflecting quietly is an action step. Other times, an appropriate action step might be to make a decision. Or, an action step may be to implement a plan developed during the coaching conversation.

There are three elements that, if included in the action step, will help the coachee be more successful in accomplishing them.

- Simple enough to complete, yet significant enough to build momentum.
- Moves the coachee toward their goal.
- Doable before the next coaching conversation.

Let's look a closer at the three elements that define an action step. First, an action step should be described as a single, identifiable action that is small enough and simple enough to complete, yet at the same time is significant enough to build momentum.

Some action steps cannot be completed in a week or two. If an action step is too large, the coachee may become lost in the complexity of it or discouraged by an unexpected turn of events as they try to implement the action. Instead, divide a too-large action step into different parts or smaller action steps. A step-by-step approach, using small relevant action steps, better supports a coachee as he or she works to accomplish them. Later in this chapter, I'll show you how to help the coachee divide a large action step into several smaller ones.

Second, many people want to reach a coaching goal in one big leap. The standard measurement of an action step is that it produces movement toward the coachee's goal, not that he or she reaches the goal immediately. Forward movement removes pressure on the coachee to "do it all" right now. Instead, it promotes an incremental approach, acknowledging that accomplishing the goal is a process that takes time. Each step forward is a small win, encouraging the coachee on to the next small win. So don't ask, "What will you do this week to accomplish your goal?" This question may create an unrealistic expectation that the coachee's entire coaching goal can be reached this week with just a few action steps. Most significant goals that require coaching are not that simple. Achieving large or complex goals requires time and effort. A better question is, "What will you do this week to move forward?"

Finally, it's best if each action step is completed before the next coaching conversation. The ongoing nature of coaching mimics the Action-Reflection Cycle. The coachee reflects and creates new action steps and then implements them. During the next coaching conversation, the coachee reviews previous action steps and creates a new plan of action. The Action-Reflection Cycle is built into the coaching process. It is important that the coachee takes action between coaching conversations. Doing so ensures the coachee will learn from these actions and reflects further.

Generate Multiple Options

As the coaching conversation progresses through the Awareness stage and into the Course stage, it is the coach's job to help coachees discover multiple options that will move them toward their larger coaching goals. Often as coachees receive some new insight on their situations, they also have ideas for what to do next. It's easy to fixate on just one idea. Or sometimes the opposite happens, and the coachee keeps looking for the magic "right answer" that will solve all their problems.

Consider Pastor Jerry's story. He had recently become the Senior Pastor of a medium-sized church. During the first six months problems began to surface: relational conflict, sin, and a history of poor financial decisions. He came to understand that the church was in a much worse financial position than he had been led to believe. Also, he discovered that there was a large group of long-time members that were ready to split off and form a new church. Jerry needed a solution to this complex situation.

As he laid out all the factors and explored different perspectives and options in the Awareness Stage, his clarity increased, but so did his understanding of the complexity of the situation. This clarity increased his frustration rather than relieving it. What Jerry wanted was "the answer" that would fix everything. He wanted something he could do now to get the church under control and moving forward in a manageable way. Yet, the complexity of the situation presented a number of possible solutions, each with strengths and weaknesses, and all of which would take time and a lot work. Jerry kept asking himself, "What is the right answer?"

In our world of increasing complexity and rapid change, it's tempting to be simplistic in our thinking. When there is a problem we look for *the right* answer. Who wouldn't want the right answer? The difficulty with "right" answer thinking is that it is all or nothing. One answer is right. All other answers are wrong. Most of life does not work this way. More often "it depends" is the answer to many of life's problems.

"Nothing is more dangerous than an
idea when it is the only one you have."
—Emilè Chartier, French philosopher

There is usually more than one right answer to life's challenges. The many variables involved produce different, and sometimes conflicting, answers. The coach's role is to help increase the coachee's perspective so that they recognize more of the variables, notice more roads to travel on, and see more options.

While there is rarely one right answer, there may be *many* right answers.[16] Note the "s" at the end of "answers." In our search for *the* right answer, we may miss answers that view things from different perspectives, answers that weigh the variables differently, and answers that fit different personalities and strengths.

Generating multiple options will provide the clearest way forward. The second or third option might be the best or "right" one. Multiple options can be compared and evaluated against one another. They can be combined to create more holistic solutions, and they can be adapted to reduce risk and mitigate against potential consequences.

To generate multiple options, use plural forms when asking. Ask for options instead of an option, answers instead of an answer, and ideas instead of an idea.

What ideas do you have?
How else might you approach this problem?
What are a couple unrealistic or crazy ideas that have crossed your mind?
What are three diverse approaches to this problem?

Options are just that—options. Don't confuse options with a commitment to action. There's a big difference between "I could do X, Y, or Z" and "I will do X." Discussing options uses language like: could, might, probably will, maybe, etc. Move from generating options to making a firm commitment to one or more of these options by asking,

Which of these options will you choose to pursue?
What will you commit to doing before our next coaching conversation?

The Power of Small Wins

You know the old joke: How do you eat an elephant? One bite at a time. As obvious as it is to eat an elephant in many small bites, we still look for ways to accomplish our big goals in just a couple of big bites. A "big bite" strategy often does not work well. Instead, create small, forward-moving action steps that build on one another. This method usually gets us to our goals faster.

Let's look at why working in small steps is helpful, and then I will show you how to divide any action step into several smaller, easy-to-accomplish steps.

Every completed action step is a win, no matter how small. The results of each small win build on each other and compound into greater results, ultimately leading the coachee to accomplish their goal. John Kotter in his book, *Leading Change,*[17] writes that small wins are critical for successful completion of a larger goal. He lists several positive benefits that make small wins advantageous.

Kotter writes that small wins:

- *Provide evidence that sacrifices are worth it:* Wins greatly help justify the short-term costs involved.

- *Reward the coachee with a pat on the back:* After a lot of hard work, positive feedback builds morale and motivation.
- *Help fine-tune vision and strategy:* Small wins give the coachee concrete data on the viability of their ideas.
- *Keep others on board:* Provides others with evidence that the goal is on track.
- *Build momentum:* Progress toward the goal is established and others are motivated to help.

Every Action Step Can Be Divided

A common mistake in forming action steps is to make them too large or complex. To take advantage of the power of small wins, multiple smaller action steps are a better way to go. It is the coach's job to help the coachee break larger action steps into smaller, more manageable steps. This way the coachee can tap into the motivational power of small wins as they work through their action steps. Let's look at how to effectively divide up action steps.

Every action step is actually made up of a number of smaller actions steps—thoughts, decisions, and actions. Allow me to illustrate with a mundane example. Imagine my action step is: "Go outside within 10 minutes." Simple enough. Most people would consider going outside within 10 minutes as a single action step. Yet, this task is actually a series of smaller steps. As I write, I am sitting at a desk on the 11th floor of the Singapore National Library,[18] so "to go outside within 10 minutes," means I must:

1. Push back my chair
2. Stand up
3. Pack up my computer
4. Walk through the library

5. Take several turns through the stacks of books
6. Open the first set of doors
7. Have my bag inspected by security
8. Go to the elevator
9. Push the down button
10. Wait for elevator
11. Board the elevator
12. Push the button for the ground floor
13. Exit the elevator
14. Walk through the lobby
15. Open the door
16. Exit the building

For most people, "to go outside within 10 minutes" is one manageable action step. However, it is actually made up of 16 smaller action steps.

The point is to make action steps doable before the next coaching conversation. Any action step can be divided as needed into several smaller steps.

Divide and Conquer

If we consider more everyday action steps, you'll see why dividing an action step into several smaller action steps might be helpful. For example, let's look at these action steps:

1. Publish this month's newsletter.
2. Hire a new web designer.
3. Prepare to preach on Sunday.

Let's say the coachee leaves the coaching conversation with these three action steps. We assume the coachee is able to organize and do these three tasks. However, if the person needed coaching about the topic that produced these action steps, they may find that as they begin to work on these action steps, they are not clear on how to accomplish them. This lack of clarity could result in the coachee not moving forward or becoming discouraged in the process of trying.

Each of the above action steps are made up of several smaller action steps. Depending on the coachee's motivation, ability, and available time, it may be better to represent each action step as multiple smaller steps rather than fewer large ones. Once divided, it may become clear that the coachee cannot accomplish it all before the next coaching conversation. Instead, spread the work out.

How do you know if an action step is too large? Ask the coachee how they will accomplish the action step. If they hesitate or say they don't know, coach them through how they will implement each one. The coachee will finish with a detailed plan to move forward with three or four mini action steps for each larger one. The accomplishment of each mini action step will motivate the coachee to keep going. This is the power of small wins.

1. Publish this month's newsletter.
   a. Write the text
   b. Gather the photos
   c. Layout the design
   d. Print and mail

2. Hire a new web designer.
   a. Write up our design needs
   b. Clarify budget
   c. Identify potential web designers
   d. Interview candidates
   e. Decide on one

3. Prepare to teach on Sunday.
   a. Decide on topic or Scripture passage
   b. Research
   c. Pray
   d. Write
   e. Practice delivery

Combine the power of small wins and a divide-and-conquer strategy to give your coachee the best chance of moving forward. Both strategies use natural forces to propel the coachee forward toward their goal.

Coaching Action Steps

The process of coaching action steps uses many of the same question-asking techniques as in the Awareness Stage. Ask clarifying questions and explore how the coachee will accomplish the action step. If you're not sure the coachee is clear on how they will do it, then ask to be walked through exactly what will be done to complete the action step. Coach through specifics along the way by connecting ideas or insights that came up earlier in the conversation.

"Do or do not. There is no try."

— Yoda

After a conversation regarding Bob's overwhelming amounts of email, he committed himself to this action step: "I will try to get my email under control." The vagueness of this action step pretty much sets Bob up for failure. If Bob were to leave with the action step in this form, chances are he would return to the next coaching conversation having made little progress in getting his email under control. Further dialogue could help Bob sharpen up his action step into something that is attainable.

Coach: What would you like to do this week to move forward?

Bob: I will try to get my email under control.

Coach: What do you mean by "under control"?

Bob: I won't be answering emails all day long. I could do my other work without constantly being distracted by emails.

Coach: How could you do this?

Bob: I could turn off the automatic check email. That would keep them from "pinging" into my inbox and distracting me.

Coach: Yes. What else?

Bob: I'm not sure.

Coach: Earlier [during the Awareness stage] you had an idea about setting specific times to answer emails.

Bob: That's right. I'd like to try that.

Coach: What would that look like?

Bob: I could check email first thing in the morning, right after lunch, and just before I leave each day.

Coach: Picture in your mind limiting yourself to just these three times each day with the email automatic check off. What do you see?

Bob: I see people calling me around 11 o'clock because I didn't answer their email within ten minutes!

Coach: (laughs) So, you go from the email pinging to the phone ringing…

Bob: Yeah. Maybe I could let people know what times I'll be answering emails.

Coach: Okay. What action steps will you commit to regarding your email?

Bob: I will turn off the automatic check email, answer emails only at 9 a.m., 1 p.m., and 4 p.m. And I'll let people know that's when I'm checking emails.
Coach: How "doable" does this feel to you?
Bob: Very! I think it will really help.

Get SMART

The dialogue between Bob and his coach illustrates how to create clear action steps. A good action step is like a mini vision statement that describes the preferred future. Properly formed action steps will motivate the coachee and will form the basis on which to evaluate learning, growth, and performance. In creating action steps, it is helpful to make them SMART:[19]

Specific—It is clear and unambiguous.
Measurable—You can observe or measure its completion.
Attainable, yet a Stretch—It is challenging, yet possible to complete.
Relevant—It is meaningful to the coachee.
Time Limited—It will be completed by a set date.

Below are examples of questions that can be used to coach a person to make their action steps SMARTer.

Specific

Action steps are best written in a clear, unambiguous ways. The action step is a description of the desired result. Move from ideas to specific actions, from general and conceptual ideas to detailed and concrete plans. This process often requires dialogue and a number of questions until an action step becomes specific.

Concretely, what does that look like?
What specifically do you want to do?

Measurable

Action steps are measurable or observable. Concrete action steps make it easier for the coachee to know what needs to be done, and to be able to recognize when the task is completed. Measurable action steps are helpful to evaluate progress more objectively.

How will you know when you've accomplished this action step?
How can you measure or observe that?
How much is enough?

Attainable, yet a Stretch

Some coachees try for too much, and some for too little. Help the coachee create doable action steps that stretch them at the same time. Challenge appropriately to help the coachee step out of their current skills and to try new ways of thinking and acting.

How challenging will this action step be for you?
What action step would move you not just a couple of steps ahead, but put you on a different level altogether?

Relevant

Action steps can be specific, measurable, and attainable, but have little relevance to the coachee's goals. Relevance means creating action steps that are meaningful to the coachee and will move toward their goal. Relevant action steps tap the inner motivation of the coachee.

How important or meaningful is this action step to you?
How does this action step relate to your goal?

Time-limited

Action steps need a deadline. A time limit increases the likelihood that the coachee will accomplish the action step. Time limits should also be attainable, yet a stretch. A stretch might be a shorter time frame, which forces the coachee to think in new ways to meet the deadline. Remember that the coaching process itself provides one level of time limit, as most action steps will be completed before the next coaching conversation.

What's your deadline for accomplishing this?
Why then, and not two weeks earlier?

Making Intangible Action Steps Tangible

Some action steps are difficult to make specific or measurable. Action steps regarding feelings, attitudes, emotions, character, temperament, and spirituality can be very difficult to make tangible. It's difficult to see, touch, taste, smell or hear a new emotion or character quality.

The process of making intangible action steps tangible involves identifying the tangible things behind an intangible goal and making those things into action steps.

Sometimes we intuitively sense change. For example, a woman may feel her husband does not love her as much as before. Her perception may be based on a number of tangible things that, individually, do not look like much—how attentive he is when they are together, his tone of voice, the number of unplanned calls, gifts, or "I love you's" he says. Together these small actions or inactions lead her to the conclusion that her husband feels differently toward her. Tangible actions are often the source of intangible feelings.

Linking an intangible action step to tangible behaviors makes the action step more specific and measurable—it can be observed—and thus is more achievable. Ask for the attitudes and behaviors behind the changes. Ask how these changes could be observed if achieved. Ask what the changes would look like. Compare these:

Example #1

Intangible Action Step: To be more loving toward my spouse.

Coaching Questions:

How would "more loving" show up in your behavior?

What would "more loving" look like?

What would be happening inside you if you were "more loving"?

Tangible Action Step: Give my spouse my full attention the hour after the kids are in bed, and plan and go out on a weekly "date."

Example #2

Intangible Action Step: I want to be more spiritual.

Coaching Questions:

What would the specific results look like if you were "more spiritual"?

What would be different about you if you were "more spiritual"?

Practically speaking, what would becoming "more spiritual" do for you?

Tangible Action Step: I will memorize Philippians 4:8 and think of it whenever I'm tempted to click through to an inappropriate Internet site.

To illustrate further, let's look at a coaching conversation just as it enters the Course stage. "I'll pray about it" is a common but intangible action step to which many Christians want to commit. Let's look at how to coach this intangible action step into something more tangible.

> Coach: What would you like to do to move forward?
> *Sue: I'm going to pray about it.*
> Coach: Okay. And what would that look like—praying every morning, a special time, or what?
> *Sue: Oh, I want to take a half-day to really listen to the Lord.*
> Coach: Where would you do this?
> *Sue: In the past, I've gone to a retreat center near my home, usually for a morning. My friend works there and lets me use a room for free.*
> Coach: I see. And when you're there what will you do?
> *Sue: I usually spend some time reading Psalms to get my mind focused on the Lord. After this, I take time to simply be quiet— sometimes for an hour. Then a conversation seems to begin and I "talk through" the issue with the Lord, often journaling about it.*
> Coach: That sounds helpful. Is this what you'd like to do?
> *Sue: Yes.*

It's tempting to stop the conversation here now that the action step is specific and measurable. Yet, read how the conversation continued to see how the SMART step of limiting time might show up in a conversation.

> Coach: When will you do this?
> *Sue: That's the question... (Pulling out her calendar) The next two weeks I am swamped!*
> Coach: (waits)
> *Sue: Well, I could do it three weeks from now.*

Coach: Would that meet your needs?

Sue: No. (sighs…) I hate having to schedule prayer!

Coach: What options do you see?

Sue: I suppose I could forget about using a whole morning for prayer. But it takes a while for me just to get focused, so I don't want to give up on that idea.

Coach: I acknowledge your effort to stick with the process that has provided perspective for you in the past. Looking at your schedule, what could possibly be rearranged in the next week so you could do this?

Sue: The best time would be Tuesday, if I changed a couple of appointments.

Coach: How doable is that?

Sue: Easy. I just hate rescheduling appointments.

Coach: What would you like to do?

Sue: I'll change them. This is too important.

Coach: What action steps will you take?

Sue: I'll change my appointments. And on Tuesday morning I will go to the retreat center to pray and journal about this issue.

Coach: What support do you need to do this?

Sue: None, I'll be able to manage it.

Coach: Okay. I look forward to hearing the results.

Creating Action Steps From Different Angles

In normal practice the coachee will leave every coaching session having identified action steps. Ask for two or three action steps for each coaching topic. If one action step cannot be completed or does not help, perhaps one of the others will meet the need.

Use questions from different angles—relational, spiritual, and organizational, etc.—to help the coachee create a holistic plan of action. Often the angles you explored together in the Awareness stage will produce ideas for action steps that consider those perspectives. Use the same process as in the Awareness stage but ask about actions.

> **How might you work on this from a relational perspective? You mentioned earlier the organizational dimensions to this issue. What could you do from that perspective?**

Examples of Action Steps

The following sets of action steps are the product of different coaching conversations. It is expected that each action step will be completed prior to the next coaching conversation, so they do not have times fixed to them.

Notice how each action step approaches the coaching topic from a different angle. In the first example, the action steps are from intellectual, relational, and spiritual angles. Different approaches will produce different types of results, so angles are important.

Each action step is not absolutely SMART. There's an art to helping make an action step SMART enough that the coachee will know how to complete it, without becoming patronizing or irritating. Help SMARTen up action steps until the coachee feels confident of their plan of action. You will both find out if they were SMART enough when you follow up on the action steps at the next coaching conversation.

Example 1

Today's Coaching Conversation Outcome: Make a plan to assess where our team is right now.

Action steps from today's coaching conversation:
- I will read John Kotter's book *Leading Change*.
- I will meet individually with Peter and Su-Jin and ask their opinion of our current team dynamics.

- I will take Tuesday morning to pray and journal regarding next steps for our team.

Example 2

Today's Coaching Conversation Outcome: Do I need an MBA?

Action steps from today's coaching conversation:
- I will fine-tune my list of reasons for pursuing an MBA.
- I will use the Internet to research nearby graduate schools with MBA programs.
- I will email the HR department to understand policies concerning using company time and money to complete an MBA program.

Example 3

Today's Coaching Conversation Outcome: Feel fit and energetic.

Action steps from today's coaching conversation:
- I will work out at the gym for 90 minutes next Monday, Wednesday, and Friday mornings.
- I will eat a salad every workday for lunch.
- I will review my "stress list"[20] every morning and pray through high score areas.

Coaching Action Steps

The various techniques for coaching action steps can be combined into a three-step dialogue. By coaching action steps, we help the coachee to think through what actions would be relevant, what they will do, how they will do it, and by when. Planning these things prior to attempting action steps provides a much greater chance of a positive result.

1. *Ask for Action Steps*

Depending on the flow of the conversation you may first ask for options or go straight to commitment to action steps.

What actions will you take to move forward?

What else would you like to do?

Prompt from different angles. For example,

Who could help you?

Earlier you mentioned X, is this something you'd like to do?

What could you do from a spiritual perspective?

2. *SMARTen Up the Action Steps*

Coach towards SMART action steps. This includes dividing any too-large action steps into several smaller steps to tap into the power of small wins.

3. *Confirm the Action Steps*

Confirm the action steps and make sure that you and the coachee have them written down. This step makes following-up on action steps much easier.

What are your action steps?

How do you feel about these action steps? [Coach around any hesitations.]

Get the Next Appointment into the Calendar

Some coaches and coachees have a consistent enough schedule to set regular days and times for their coaching conversations, every Tuesday at 10 a.m. for example. My coachees and I do not. Travel, meetings, kid's sports, etc., make it difficult to predict a regular schedule a month or two in advance. No problem. Set the time and date for the next coaching appointment at the end of creating action steps and before Highlights. Doing this in-person is much easier than exchanging emails later.

Coach: How about we set our next coaching appointment?
Coachee: Sure.
Coach: Are you available 2 p.m. on Tuesday the 10th?
Coachee: That works for me.

This brings us to the end of Course. From here you'll ask the coachee for Highlights, which is covered in the next chapter.

Conclusion

The purpose of action steps is to help coachees successfully apply their insights and discoveries from the coaching conversation. Insights paired with action steps will produce the progress coachees hope to see.

Action steps should be simple, they should move coachees toward their goals, and be doable before the next coaching conversation. To begin coaching action steps, ask for multiple options. Help them generate a number of ideas, then have them narrow the action steps down and commit to taking action. Divide any large or complex action steps into small steps to tap into the power of small wins. Use SMART to help coachees make plans that will better prepare them to succeed. Turn intangible action steps into tangible ones by examining behaviors. For a balanced approach, look for multiple action steps from different angles.

The coaching conversation wraps up with one final brief stage—Highlights. Read on to learn how to create a powerful conclusion.

Highlights

"...for it is God who works in you to will
and to act in order to fulfill his good purpose."
—Philippians 2:13

The coaching conversation is now at the final stage. Take a few moments at the end of your conversation to give the coachee an opportunity to summarize what he or she has learned and state it succinctly. This will cement the learning in the coachee's mind and give the coach valuable feedback at the same time.

Make it Memorable

Pastor Arty was on the edge of burnout. The church that he started three years earlier had grown to a hundred regularly participating members, including many people who came to faith through the ministry. Pastor

Arty struggled to keep up with the discipleship, counseling, and leadership needs of this group of new Christians. He worked at training older believers to care for the others, only to find that these believers had as many emotional and spiritual issues as the new believers. He was overwhelmed.

Pastor Arty and his coach talked through the situation from many different perspectives and came up with a number of options for moving forward. After Arty settled on two action steps, the coach concluded with the question, "What do you want to remember from this conversation?"

Pastor Arty looked up and thoughtfully replied, "I want to remember that I'm not Superman. I'm not responsible for the world and cannot meet everyone's needs."

This was one of those cool coaching moments. Superman had not been mentioned during the coaching conversation. Pastor Arty created this metaphor as he summarized the coaching conversation. It became quite memorable.

A few days later, Pastor Arty posted a photo of himself on Facebook wearing a tee shirt with a Superman symbol on the front with a big X through it. As Pastor Arty continued to work through his challenges over the next nine months, his "No Superman" metaphor continued to surface during coaching conversations.

Cement the learning in the coachee's mind by asking a Highlights question.

Finish Strong

No one likes a conversation with an awkward conclusion or unclear ending. Sometimes it's difficult to know how long is long enough.

Highlights provide a clear closure to the coaching conversation. A summary of the conversation completes it like tying a ribbon on a gift.

Highlights have tremendous learning value as well. Highlights give the coachee a chance to simplify the complexity of an hour-long conversation into a few short statements. It cements the coachee's learning, and also provides the coach with valuable feedback about what the coachee found significant during the conversation.

Simplify Complexity

Asking the coachee for Highlights encourages her to review an hour-long discussion and summarize the valuable points and lessons in a few sentences. In summarizing, the coachee must simplify the complexity of all the twists and turns of the conversation and sort out what was most important or meaningful for her.

Before I started wrapping up my coaching conversations with Highlights, I overheard someone I had just coached trying to tell his colleague about our coaching conversation. The coachee answered enthusiastically, "It was really helpful!" His colleague asked what was helpful. The coachee stammered, "Uh, lots of things. We talked through all kinds of things. I'm really encouraged!"

The coachee was encouraged by our coaching conversation but couldn't repeat the main points of his learning. After hearing that vague summary of our coaching conversation, I realized that he might have become lost in the complexity of our conversation. To summarize requires a fairly high degree of clarity. As Albert Einstein said, "If you can't explain it simply, you don't understand it well enough." Educationally, I knew this meant he was not clear on what we had accomplished during our conversation and had not internalized his learning. As a coach, this meant that I wasn't doing my job well enough.

Summarize to Build Your Brain

Learning is reinforced through a succinct summary. Which is easier to remember: three paragraphs of text or three bullet points? A bullet point is a concise summary of something that is described more fully elsewhere. A summary of a coaching conversation is easier to remember, and therefore easier to share with others. And sharing with others is important, because repeating it further reinforces the learning.

Here's how it works. Our brain continues to develop into adulthood, having the capacity to grow and rewire itself throughout our lives. This ability is called "neuroplasticity."[21] Each time you think, do, or say something, your brain sends a signal along a neural pathway. The more signals that travel along a particular pathway, the stronger that pathway becomes. Literally, we build our brains by repeating things. This is the science behind the saying that to create a new habit you must do something 16 times.

The trouble is, new neural pathways are weak, and what's worse, our brain tends to default to older, stronger pathways that we might not want it to use. It takes some mental effort to force our brains to use the new pathway. As a neural pathway is strengthened, it is easier to remember our new learning and live it out. Summarizing learning and then sharing it with others cements the learning, rewiring our brains in the process.

Summarizing learning and then sharing it with others
cements the learning, rewiring our brains in the process.

Learn What The Coachee Values

Highlights serve as a mini feedback mechanism for the coach. As the coachee expresses what they found valuable during the coaching conversation, the coach receives valuable feedback.

At the end of our second coaching session, I asked Alison, a team leader in South East Asia, what was most meaningful for her from our coaching conversation. I thought she would mention the plan that we had outlined for her team. At the beginning of our conversation she was confused. She felt like there were too many options, not enough money, and she saw no solution. By the end of the conversation, she had outlined major points of a plan to move her ministry team forward over the next 12 months. She seemed excited and relieved to have some clarity, but that's not what she mentioned when I asked what part of our conversation was most meaningful to her. She replied, "I'm just happy to have someone who will listen to me. No one listens to me."

This little piece of information spoke volumes about Alison's needs. I took note and, in subsequent coaching conversations, made doubly sure that I allowed her plenty of time to fully express her thoughts, ideas, and dreams. A Highlights question revealed her need to be listened to.

Ask It, Don't Say It

I've heard some new coaches summarize the coachee's learning at the end of the coaching conversation. Besides being presumptuous, this misses the point of Highlights. Highlights are for the coachee to summarize, not the coach.

I can understand why a coach might do this. We run a risk in asking for Highlights. What if the coachee says they had no new insights, inspirations, or anything memorable? That might be awkward. It is less risky to tell the coachee what, in your view, are the learning points. But, coaching is about drawing out, not putting in. It is our job to draw out what the coachee learned and found valuable, not what we think was valuable.

Highlights Questions

There are many ways to ask for Highlights. Each question may draw out something slightly different. Each will stimulate thinking and get to the point of summarizing what was helpful or important to the coachee.

I usually only ask one of these at the end of a coaching conversation. Try asking different Highlights questions throughout the coaching relationship.

What do you want to remember from today's conversation?
What awareness do you have now that you didn't before?
What was most useful to you from our conversation?
What are your take-aways from this conversation?
What was meaningful to you from our conversation?

The coachee's thoughts must be clear to be easily remembered. It may take a little exploration to help the coachee organize their thoughts and put them into sentences. A short dialogue using clarifying questions will help the coachee process their Highlights.

Coach: What was meaningful to you from our conversation?
Coachee: The discussion of my priorities.
Coach: How was that meaningful?
Coachee: I realized that what I say I want to do and how I actually spend my time are quite different.
Coach: Keep going.

Coachee: Well, it's not really a time-management issue as much as it is clarifying what I really want and keeping it in front of me. I'm hopeful I can make some progress this week.
Coach: I am too!

This brings us to the end of the coaching conversation. From here the coachee will go and work on their action steps. A week or two later the coach and coachee will meet again for another coaching conversation.

Follow-Up

"When the apostles returned, they
reported to Jesus what they had done."
—Luke 9:10a

A t the conclusion of most coaching conversations, the coachee commits to a number of action steps, which are to be completed before the next coaching session. Ideally, the coachee will have two or three action steps that help them move toward their goal from different angles. You can read more about creating action steps in the chapter on Course.

It is best to follow up on action steps during the Connect stage of the next coaching conversation. Following-up on action steps is critical to the overall learning process. It is at this point that the Action-

Reflection Cycle comes full circle, and each subsequent coaching conversation repeats the cycle again. Figure 3 illustrates how after a coaching conversation the coachee does action steps, then at the next conversation those action steps are followed up, and so on.

The purpose of following-up is to debrief the coachee on actions taken. This process helps to reinforce forward-moving thoughts and behaviors, generates learning and insight, and allows the coach and coachee to troubleshoot difficulties while creating next steps.

As you make a habit of following-up on action steps, you embed subtle accountability into the process. A coachee's motivation for completing action steps is naturally increased just by knowing that the coach will be following-up on them.

COACHING CONVERSATIONS AND ACTION CYCLE

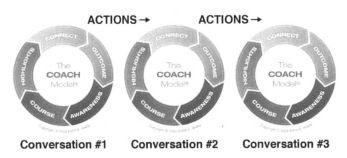

Figure 3: Coaching Conversations and Action Cycle

Safe Follow-Up

Following-up on action steps provides space for the coachee to review their actions, and the results of those actions, all in a safe environment. By safe, I am referring to the emotional safety that is a product of the coach's non-judgmental presence. People are very savvy when it comes to picking up on the judgment of others. If we perceive we are being judged negatively, we often become defensive and decline to share further.

Even positive judgments need to be tempered. While coaching, we want to keep the focus on the coachee's agenda, efforts, and accomplishments, not on how *we* evaluate their progress. We do not want to inadvertently communicate to the coachee that they are to try and please us by accomplishing their action steps. The coachee should be taking action steps for their own benefit, not for the benefit of the coach.

All forward movement needs to be reinforced so that the coachee feels encouraged to continue with these positive actions. Be generous with your acknowledgement. The words you use to acknowledge a coachee's progress make a difference in how effectively it reinforces the coachee's behavior. Phrases like, "Great job!" "I like it," and "Brilliant!" are more like pep phrases if they are not tied to any specific attitude or behavior. Instead use phrases like these, which focus on the coachee's actions:

I recognize the tremendous amount of effort you put into that.

You did it! You accomplished _____ exactly as you set out to do.

I acknowledge how much courage it took for you to do this.

The coachee is fully responsible for their action steps. Following-up with them in an empowering way will further promote that responsibility and motivate them to achieve more.

The First Following-up Question

Compare the three questions below. What characterizes them in your view? Which do you like better? Why?

Did you do your action steps?
How did it go with your action steps?
What progress did you make on your action steps?

Did you do your action steps?
This question reminds me of the question, "Did you do your homework?" Who asks that? Your parents or a teacher—an authority figure. Coaches are not authority figures. Our purpose in following-up is not to check up on the coachee, it's to support them in learning and moving forward.

"Did you do your action steps?" is a closed question. Possible responses include "Yes," "No," and "Not completely." None of these answers move the coachee towards greater reflection.

If action steps were not completed entirely, this question may raise feelings of guilt or shame, or the coachee may become defensive and make excuses. These responses decrease the coachee's ability to reflect clearly and learn from their incomplete action step.

How did it go with your action steps?
This question is usually interpreted as an evaluation, i.e., "How would you evaluate the results?" Often the answer is a simplistic, single-word assessment of a possibly complex result. The coachee may answer, "Fine" or "Great!" or "Terrible." These responses do not indicate much reflection.

In East Asia, where I lived for 20 years, if you ask, "How did it go?" the average person will list the problems and improvements needed. Their focus is generally on self-critiquing rather than on the "build on strengths" approach common in the United States.[22] Some personalities in the United States will give the same self-critiquing response. Following-up on action steps involves more than correcting the execution of action steps.

The biggest disadvantage to beginning with this question is that it provides no reinforcement for what was successful. In Indonesia, I worked with a leader who was quick to self-evaluate and find places he needed to improve. He worked diligently on those areas, but I soon began to notice that he was doing poorly in areas where he had previously done well. I realized that by not reinforcing his effective behaviors, he began to see those behaviors as unimportant and therefore did not continue them. Reinforcing all forward movement is important so that the coachee will continue with those positive behaviors.

I find it more helpful to evaluate the effectiveness of the coachee's efforts after he has described his actions and their results, as illustrated in this next question.

Reinforcing all forward movement is important so the coachee will continue with those positive behaviors.

What progress did you make on your action steps?
This question, like an onion, has many layers to it. On the surface it's quite positive. Progress is assumed, and that projects a positive belief in the coachee's ability to act. It says, "I believe in you."

The word "progress" is not an all or nothing proposition as in the question, "Did you do your action steps?" Instead, "progress" includes and welcomes partially completed action steps.

"Progress" sets the conversation off in a positive direction. It focuses on what went well, what worked, and on the coachee's forward movement. It creates space for the coachee to review and reinforce forward-moving behaviors and thinking, and to cement them into his or her life. This term doesn't restrict the conversation to include only the positive results but paints any result in a positive and constructive light. More importantly, the question doesn't raise defensiveness, and most people appreciate its constructive positivism.

I used to feel awkward when following-up on action steps. I worried about appearing too authoritarian. I worried that the coachee had not completed their action steps. I worried about embarrassing them or offering ineffective help if the action steps didn't go well. Since using the question, "What progress did you make on your action steps?," my worries have disappeared.

What? So What? Now What?

Now that we have the first question ready, let's look at how to follow-up in an empowering way that will focus on learning, and motivate the coachee towards further action.

A simple model for following-up on action steps is: What? So What? Now What?[23] This model allows you to naturally explore to find out what the coachee did, didn't do, and the result (What?). From there, the model encourages deeper reflection for the purpose of discovering the lessons to be learned from those actions and results (So What?). And finishes by extending that learning into other areas of the coachee's life (Now What?). Plus, it's easy to remember, and that counts for a lot when you are in the moment with someone.

What?

Questions help the coachee review and reflect on what she did and didn't accomplish in regard to her action steps. The *What?* step is designed to raise the coachee's awareness and make her conscious of her thoughts, emotions, and behaviors before and during the action step. This requires the coachee to dig below the surface to identify many aspects of what happened. For example: what she did, what she choose not to do, what her thought process was, and what emotions were evoked as she did all of this.

Surprisingly, some people do not recognize what they have accomplished or its significance. The coachee may not be aware of the thought process that brought them to complete the action step.

Of course, not all action steps require this depth of reflection. Following-up on some action steps is simply a matter of asking about them and hearing a quick summary. Other actions steps require more exploration to discover the wisdom behind them. Action steps that were something new, a challenge, or key to the coachee reaching their goal, need more time to process.

Through the coach's questions the coachee is able to be more fully aware of what actually happened—their actions, internal conversations, emotions—and the results. Reflecting with this much detail makes it easier for the coachee to discover new learning.

For example, Martin worked for a large relief organization and needed to give a presentation to a large group of managers. During his previous presentation, in his nervousness and desire not to miss anything, he did a "data dump," droning on and on with charts and statistics that put everyone to sleep. After that poor presentation and more than a little bit of teasing from his co-workers, he was even more nervous about an upcoming presentation. We coached about how to do things differently. He created several action steps and did the presentation.

At our next coaching conversation, I followed-up on his progress. In the dialogue below, notice how I probed for what he did, how he felt, and what happened as a result of doing the action steps.

Coach: What progress did you make on your action steps?
Martin: I did the presentation, and it went well.
Coach: I realize you put a lot of work into overcoming your difficulties in presenting. What did you do differently this time?
Martin: I was better prepared.
Coach: How did you prepare differently?
Martin: I was much clearer on the purpose of the talk, so my points were more focused. I also got rid of most of the text on the PowerPoint slides and illustrated each point with photos instead. The other managers really liked that.

Coach: Okay, so you decided on a clear purpose for the presentation, focused your main points, and created an interesting PowerPoint. Nice job. How did you feel as you actually did the presentation?

Martin: I was still nervous, but I knew exactly what I was going to say, and I knew that I wouldn't ramble on and on like last time.

Coach: Besides nervousness, what emotions did you feel?

Martin: Well, I was excited... also much more confident. And I anticipated good results.

Coach: What did you do that caused those feelings?

Martin: Having clear purpose and points. I wasn't overwhelmed with all the data or worried about trying to cram ten points into the presentation time.

[This conversation is continued below under So What?]

The What? Stage explores what the coachee did or didn't do, what they thought about, what they felt, and the effects of it all. Below are some key questions:

Do: What did you do? Or not do?
Think: What did you think about as you did it?
Feel: What feelings did you have during the experience?
Effect: What were the effects of having taken these actions?

So What?

Helpful reflection goes beyond simply what happened, to the meaning behind the experience.

Ask about the implications of taking this action step, looking for both effects and process. Look for logical connections between thoughts, emotions, actions and their effects. The *effects* are the immediate results related to the action step itself, and *process* includes the new thoughts, behaviors, and experiences involved in accomplishing it.

Ask what conclusions the coachee can draw from all of this. Encourage the coachee to summarize his or her observations, insights or learning for the purpose of reinforcing it and making it easier to remember. Insights and discoveries more often come from the process, yet coachees often overlook this area.

Let's go back to Martin and his presentation.

[Continued from above...]

Coach: What do you observe about how your preparation relates to a successful presentation?

Martin: They are totally linked. Once I was clear on my purpose for the talk, it became easier to decide which points to focus on. I could also keep it more concise and stop doing the "data dump" that I used to do.

Coach: How will you prepare in the future?

Martin: Well, first I'll determine the purpose, then sort through the information to find my focus points. And I'll stick to that, rather than trying to say all there is to say about the topic.

Coach: And how does even thinking about preparing in this way make you feel about doing your next presentation?

Martin: Much more confident. I'm not dreading it.

Below are some key questions:

What did you learn? Relearn?
What benefits did you receive from this experience?
How do you feel about yourself?
What are the implications of doing this action?

Now What?

At this point, the coachee has a clear picture of what he did and the results of doing it. He has also generated insights and learning from the experience. Now we want to reinforce that learning by extending it into other areas of his life. The simplest way is to do this is to help the coachee find other applications for his insights and learning.

[Continued from above…]

Coach: How could you use your insights to prepare a clear purpose and focused points in other areas of your job?

Martin: Our staff meetings could use a lot more focus. I'm too scattered in what we talk about, and we end up leaving the meeting feeling like we ran through a checklist of unrelated things.

Coach: How might you prepare differently for your meetings?

Martin: Well, the same way as the presentation, I suppose. I need to decide on a purpose for those meetings. Do I want to inform? Inspire? Equip? A little of all three? That's the first step anyway.

Coach: Would you like to commit that to an action step?

Martin: Sure, I'll think through the purpose or purposes of our next staff meeting and make it clear.

Coach: Sounds helpful. [Pause] Is it okay if we move on to review your other action steps? [Or, if that was the last or only action step to follow-up on, set the Outcome for the rest of the session.] Looking toward the rest of our time together today, what would you like to work on?

Below are some key questions:

How can you extend the learning?
Where else could you apply what you've learned?
How do you want to do things differently in the future?

Martin's story is a good example of following-up on action steps that were completed and went well. Next, we will look at how to follow-up when the action steps were not completed or worse, failed.

Why We All Need A Little Failure Now and Then

Failure is an emotionally charged word. Its constant companion is discouragement. The word failure has a note of finality or completeness. Black or white. Bad or good. Many people fear failure, but some kinds of failure are actually good for us. Here are two reasons why a little failure now and then will make us stronger.

Failure leads to living out our potential. Some people go to great lengths not to fail. On the surface, that's understandable. However, by aiming for only what is attainable, you risk staying firmly in the grasp of mediocrity. A pole vaulter only knows her upper limit by consistently not clearing the bar. In sports, as well as work, you can only reach your potential by pushing your limits. Goals must be challenging, and that means we must risk failure.

Failure can also lead to learning. The greatest learning (or at least most memorable learning) often comes from failure. I'm from Seattle, where throughout the past 20 years, Venture Capitalists (VCs) have sought out software entrepreneurs to fund their startup companies. One factor that VCs look for is failure. Has the entrepreneur failed? If they haven't failed, some VCs do not want to fund them. Venture Capitalists know that all entrepreneurs *will* fail, and that they will gain a lot of valuable learning from that failure—but they would rather that they fail first with somebody else's money![24]

"Success consists of going from failure
to failure without loss of enthusiasm."
—Winston Churchill

Failure occurs all the time in both big and small ways. A failed action step should be viewed as a valuable learning experience. If nothing has been learned, the person is likely to repeat their error, often with more severe consequences. Following-up can help people learn from what went wrong and find and reinforce all that went right.

How to Follow-up on Failed or Incomplete Action Steps

Coachees will not fully complete every action step every time, and that's okay. Sometimes the action step wasn't specific enough, or the coach may have imposed their idea as an action step. There may have been changes in the coachee's circumstances, a crisis, or other demands of life that distracted the coachee. Or it's possible that the coachee just fell flat.

Progress in coaching is measured by what the coachee accomplishes *and* by what the coachee learns. Following-up on incomplete action steps is a chance for the coachee to increase self-awareness and learning, as well as to make corrections leading to successful completion of their goals.

The process of following-up on failed or incomplete action steps is similar to the pattern of What? So What? Now What? The key to following-up on incomplete action steps is not to move too quickly towards correcting what didn't work, but rather, taking time to review any forward progress. It's important to find and reinforce all forward movement before diagnosing and fixing what didn't work.

Of course, you must first give an empathetic ear to what may be a disappointing and discouraging result for the coachee—then focus on helping them see the progress they made.

The steps below outline how to effectively help a coachee process a failed or incomplete action step. This kind of detail won't be necessary for every situation, but it works well for those important action steps that didn't work out as a coachee had intended.

1. Dissect the action steps to identify the parts that worked and the parts that didn't work. Look for what the coachee did well.

2. Acknowledge all the forward-moving thoughts, decisions, and actions. Don't let discouragement cause the person to miss the parts that they did well.

3. Capture the learning in the same way that was described in the "So What" step above.

4. Have the coachee identify what didn't work and reflect on the causes, as well as on alternatives. Focus on what the coachee did or didn't do, and look at factors that may have been outside the coachee's control.

5. Find out if the action step is still relevant and needs to be completed.

6. Make a revised plan of action.

Dissect the Action Step

Every action step is actually made up of a large number of smaller actions steps—thoughts, decisions, and actions. Let's revisit the example of the action step from the chapter on Course: "Go outside within 10 minutes." Most people would consider "going outside within 10 minutes" as a single action step. Yet, as we saw, this action step actually required a series of 16 smaller steps for me to go outside from the 11th floor of the Singapore National Library. Here they are:

1. Push back my chair
2. Stand up
3. Pack up my computer
4. Walk through the library
5. Take several turns through the stacks of books
6. Open the first set of doors
7. Have my bag inspected by security

8. Go to the elevator
9. Push the down button
10. Wait for elevator
11. Board the elevator
12. Push the button for the ground floor
13. Exit the elevator
14. Walk through the lobby
15. Open the door
16. Exit the building

This action step actually requires 16 smaller steps, just to go outside. Now imagine that on the way down the elevator stops midway. I'm stuck, and time is up. I failed to achieve the action step. If we measure action steps as pass or fail, all or nothing, then the entire attempt at this action step is a failure. However, if we measure action steps according to *any forward movement toward the goal*, then I achieved quite a lot—12 out of 16 mini-steps. While the overall result may not have been what I hoped for, many of the individual actions moved me toward my goal.

Reinforcing these mini-actions creates powerful momentum for the coachee. Otherwise, in their disappointment over not achieving their full goal, the coachee may "throw the baby out with the bath water" by disregarding their forward movement. When following-up on action steps, don't overlook successful, forward-moving thoughts, decisions, and actions. Reinforce all forward-moving behaviors and generate learning from the parts that that did and didn't work.

Reinforce all forward-moving behaviors and generate
learning from the parts that that did and didn't work.

Let's look at the process of dissecting an action step.

The following dialogue illustrates how a coach followed-up with Danielle, who was searching for a new job and came to the coaching appointment discouraged because she felt she hadn't accomplished anything that week. Notice how the coach probes for the mini-steps and then literally points out progress to the discouraged coachee.

Coach: What progress did you make on your action steps?

Danielle: I didn't do anything this week.

Coach: Nothing?

Danielle: Nothing.

Coach: You were going to send out your résumé. How far did you get on that?

Danielle: Well, I sent it to two people, but when I called them they weren't able to meet with me until this week.

Coach: So, wait a minute. You did send your résumé to two people and you phoned them for appointments. That's big! You've been so nervous about phoning to follow-up. Great job.

Danielle: Yeah, I guess I did do something.

Coach: Yes, you did! What else?

Danielle: I spent a couple hours looking at online job-search forums. And I checked in with my friend who's a manager at Microsoft, but there was nothing available in her department.

Coach: I want to acknowledge your effort, especially when you were faced with some discouraging results.

Danielle: Thanks.

Coach: You've been job-hunting for a couple of months now. What observations can you make about the process of finding your new job?

Danielle: I see that personally following-up by phone is essential. I wouldn't even get called back if all I did was send in my résumé.

Also, I don't think it's enough for me to stick to the places I've been looking. I need to cast my net wider.

Coach: Those are helpful observations: always contact the employer personally and widen the scope of your search. [Pause] So, how would you like to use the remainder of our conversation?

[From here the coach and coachee would begin to set the Outcome for the rest of the coaching conversation.]

The coach uncovered the actions Danielle had taken and acknowledged them. Danielle hadn't yet attained the result she wanted, but the steps she did take eventually allowed her to find the job she was searching for. Below are some examples of how to genuinely acknowledge a person's effort, even if they haven't achieved the result for which they hoped.

You obviously put tremendous thought into that.

I acknowledge your willingness to try. I know it wasn't easy for you.

I recognize this was quite a stretch for you, but you showed courage and went for it. I respect that.

In the example above, you can also find the "So What" step of following-up. Here the coach used it as a review of the coachee's efforts to date. Those insights may inform the coaching conversation and future action steps.

What did you learn from what you did?

Looking at what you did do, what do want to make sure you do again?

Revise the Action Step

Create a new revised action step that considers past difficulties. Use insights from the coachee's recent experience to plan a way forward. It's a two-step process. First, assess the coachee's commitment to complete the action step, and second, reform the action step in light of the coachee's learning.

Assess the Coachee's Commitment to the Action Step

Before charging ahead and assuming the coachee will complete the action step in the upcoming weeks, stop and ask if the action step is still relevant.

There are a number of reasons an action step may no longer be needed. Circumstances change, the completion of other action steps may have accomplished the original intention, or new insights may have given the coachee a different approach to the problem. Occasionally a coachee will decide on an action step, and later realize it's not a priority.

The simplest way to assess the coachee's continued commitment to the action step is by asking. Try one of these questions:

How important is it to you to complete this action step?
How relevant is this action step to you now?
In what ways will completing this action move you toward your goal?

Assessing commitment to the action step gives the coachee a chance to connect to their original motivations for creating the action step in the first place. It's not uncommon to hear answers such as, "I've got to complete it!" or "I don't have any choice, really. It's essential to the project." Most of the time the coachee will want to continue with the action step.

There will be times when the coachee decides that completing the action step is not necessary. Although there's room for variation, the three main reasons for not continuing with an action step are as follows: one or more of the other action steps met the intentions of the uncompleted action step, circumstances changed making it irrelevant, or the coachee wasn't clear or committed to the action step from the beginning.

If the coachee does not want to continue with the action step, move on to debriefing the other action steps and then transition to determining the Outcome of the remainder of that day's coaching conversation.

If the coachee is committed to accomplishing the action step, continue and have a brief conversation about how to reform the action step to make it more relevant.

Reform the Action Step

During the previous coaching conversation, the coachee created an action step. The coachee attempted to accomplish the action step and then debriefed that attempt with you. Based on the coachee's experience and insights, and because of the coachee's continued commitment to accomplish it, coach them to create a plan for successful completion of the action step. Often this involves modifying the action step in some way.

Ask this key question:

In what ways does the action step need to be changed?

From this point, the conversation is similar to the process of setting new action steps. Is it SMART enough? Troubleshoot the action step based on the information and learning that emerged earlier from discussing What? and So What? Here are some other helpful questions:

Too big:

Would it be helpful to break the action step down into smaller steps?

Too Small:

How could you change the action step in such a way that you have to stretch yourself to achieve it?

Not in the Coachee's Control:

What part do you have the ability to complete? Where could you get help for the rest?

"Life" Got in the Way:

What do you need to do in order to work this action step into your busy schedule?
Would it be helpful for you to have a conversation around the pressures you're experiencing in your schedule?

With the action step debriefed and revised, the coachee is more prepared to accomplish it. Your attention to the follow-up process will ensure a greater chance of success for the coachee. The purpose of coaching is to help people succeed in the tasks and areas of responsibility to which God has called them.

Move to the Conversation Outcome

During an intentional coaching conversation, connecting by chit-chatting and following-up on action steps usually lasts only a few minutes. It can be tempting at times to continue talking about these things, as so many interesting topics may emerge.

Up to this point in the conversation, you have been reviewing the past, finding out how the coachee is doing, and following-up on action steps. Now it's time to change the focus to the future by asking the coachee an Outcome question. This approach gives you both the ability to shift the conversation to what the coachee would like to work on that day.

After following-up on action steps, pause and summarize, and then ask an Outcome question.

> **You've made great progress on your actions steps! As we move forward, what result would you like to take away from our conversation?**
> **It's very cool how you were able to _____ and _____.**
> **[pause] How would you like to use the remainder of our time together today?**
> **We could continue talking about this if you would like, but let's pause for a moment and clarify what you would like to work on today.**

Each example shows how to transition from reviewing the past action steps, to moving the conversation into the future. From this point, use the process described in the chapter on Outcome to determine the coachee's priorities for the conversation.

Conclusion

If done well, Follow-Up is one of the most productive parts of the coaching conversation. Many people learn by doing. Asking them to reflect on what they did and what they learned from it can produce more insights and discoveries than they experience in the Awareness stage of the conversation.

Following-up on action steps provides a natural accountability that motivates people to push harder than they might have on their own. Starting with the question "What progress did you make on your action steps?" is a positive way to begin. The coachee can celebrate accomplishment, as well as receive an empathetic ear.

Looking for learning in the coachee's experience, whether things went as he or she expected or not, moves the experience from doing, to learning and reflection. Incomplete or failed action steps are an opportunity for the coach to acknowledge any forward progress and for the coachee to learn from their experience. Asking the coachee how important it is to complete the action steps provides an indicator of the coachee's commitment to moving forward with that particular step. Revise the action steps as needed.

Once you've followed-up on action steps, transition to Outcome and ask the coachee how they would like to use the remainder of the conversation.

Coaching Others

"Two are better than one, because they have a good return for
their labor: if either of them falls down, one can help the other up.
But pity anyone who falls and has no one to help them up."
Ecclesiastes 4:9-10

Using The COACH Model® In Daily Conversations

The word "coach" is both a noun and a verb. To be a Coach *(noun)* is to have the position, role, or title of Coach. Some people seek qualifications and titles, thinking that once they've acquired these things, they will be ready and able to coach others. Professional level coaching training will provide tremendous benefit, but coaching is not about the certificates—it's about helping others gain perspective and take action.

We have conversations every day. Most of them are not coaching conversations. They are brief interactions on-the-go. Remember, if you change your conversations, you'll change your results. So, just coach *(verb)* people! You can build stronger relationships and see people excel by incorporating elements of The COACH Model® into your everyday conversations.

Meeting regularly provides the best help to people, regardless of how proficient you are in your new coaching skills. Don't worry about using all five steps of The COACH Model® for every conversation. Use whatever part of the model is helpful to that person and that conversation.

In normal conversations, listen well. Be curious, even if you think you already "know." Ask questions. Ask about the other person's ideas before jumping in to share your own. Finish conversations or meetings by asking, "What could you do to move forward with this?"

Here are more ideas on how to specifically use the five steps of The COACH Model® to improve your daily conversations at work and at home:

Connect. *Build rapport and trust.*
People love to talk! Everyone feels valued and important when someone listens and pays attention to them. Ask a question, and really listen. Continue with additional questions to encourage the person to share more. Asking an employee, "How was your weekend?," isn't meaningless small talk. It's a chance to learn what they value and how they feel about their lives right now.

- Ask a co-worker, "How are things at home?"
- After an event, ask your spouse, "Who did you connect with the most?"
- Ask an employee, "What was the best part of your weekend?"

Outcome. *Draw out what's on the other person's mind.*
In every conversation you have an agenda. Maybe you want to be heard or to pass on information or get something done. You know your agenda, but what's the other person's agenda? If you know what's on their mind, it will be much easier to communicate and work together or enjoy time together.

- Ask an employee, "What would be helpful to you for us to talk about?"
- Ask your supervisor, "What result would you like from our meeting today?"
- Ask your spouse, "What do you want to make sure we do this weekend?"

You know your agenda, but what's the other person's agenda? Find out by asking!

Awareness. *Encourage exploration, discovery, and shifts of perspective.*
In our fast-paced world we too often cut short conversations that require exploration. We're looking for easy answers that don't create more work. Instead, encourage exploration by asking questions that will cause the other person to reflect more deeply. Then you'll find underlying issues, meaning, and new learning.

- Ask your coworker, "What other factors might be affecting this situation?"
- Ask an employee, "From the customer's perspective, what do you think they are seeing?"

- Ask your teenager, "What do you hope will happen if you join that event / sport / club?"

Course. *Form insights into 2 or 3 actionable steps.*
Insights without action steps are just good ideas. Rather than telling someone what you'd like them to do, invite them to action by asking them what they will do next. When you give people a choice to do something, they feel more ownership and are more likely to complete it.

- Ask an employee, "What actions could you take to move forward on this?"
- Ask your child, "What are the next couple of steps in working on that project?"
- Finish a meeting by asking, "What will each of us commit to do before our next meeting?"

Insights without action steps are just good ideas.

Highlights. *Deepen reflection and surface learning.*
Every day we have experiences, but we don't always learn from them. In fact, because we don't reflect deeply enough on our experiences we gain very little from them. Instead, ask a Highlights question to encourage deeper thinking. Listen for insights, lessons, principles, and learning to bubble up to the surface.

- When an employee shares an experience, ask, "What did you learn about yourself through this?"
- As you finish reading something ask yourself, "What was most useful from this article?"

- At the dinner table ask, "What do you want to remember from today?"

Coaching skills can be used in any situation, one skill at a time. Don't wait until you have time or the perfect situation to put the whole COACH Model® all together into a long conversation.

Using Coaching Skills With Your Children

As I wrote at the beginning of this book, I learned to coach just as my two children entered their teenage years. I became better at integrating coaching skills into my parenting approach each year. Which was fortunate for me, and them.

As a parent, you don't change to the role of Coach with your children, but you can use a coaching style of interaction. At a basic level, this means moving from statements to questions. Asking instead of advising.

Kids want help with their problems, but they don't want to be fixed. The key is to keep your conversations casual. You can engage them in "undercover" coaching conversations to help them reflect and possibly create some steps forward. Tone down your inner problem solver and be empathetic. Again, don't worry about using all of The COACH Model®. It's much more important to listen well, then ask great questions.

Let me give an example of how one mother used coaching skills with her teenage son.

Teen: I'm so stressed!
Mom: What's up?
Teen: There's a history paper due Friday. (Today is Wednesday.)
Mom: What are you writing about? (Rather than trying to correct him by asking when the assignment was originally given and why he hasn't been working on it up till now.)

Teen: I'm thinking about how the U.S. Constitution was both unique and built on other documents when it was written.

Mom: How is that going?

Teen: I haven't done much on it yet.

Mom: What's your plan to complete it? (Yet again, resisting temptation to lecture about not starting earlier.)

Teen: I've got most of the research completed but can't get started writing. (Ah, he's done more than Mom thought...)

Mom: What's holding you back?

Teen: I'm not sure where to start.

Mom: If you think of your paper as a movie, how would you tell the story of the Constitution?

Teen: Well, I'd start with the situation before the Constitution was written, highlighting the freedoms and lack of freedoms of the Colonists. I suppose I could try and match the freedoms to existing documents like the Magna Carta.

Mom: Great! What happens next?

Teen: I could finish with the unique points of the Constitution and give examples of what these points have meant to people in the United States.

Mom: That sounds like an outline for an excellent history paper! (Affirming progress, and not adding her own ideas.)

Teen: Yeah, I better write that down.

Mom: I'm around tonight if I can help in any way.

Teen: Thanks mom.

Imagine how different this conversation would have been if the mother had lectured her son about waiting until the last minute to start on his paper. It would have erupted into a fight with the teenager stomping off to his room, angry, and further than ever from finishing his history paper.

Instead, as the conversation progressed, his mom found out that he actually had done quite a bit of research. She used the Outcome process to identify where in the process her son was stuck and helped him come up with a plan (Awareness, then Course) based on his own ideas.

Did she begin with the Outcome question, "What result would you like to take away from our conversation?" No. The result her son wanted was clear enough. She helped him to troubleshoot the problem and come up with next steps. If he becomes stuck again, he is more likely to go to her because she empowered him to move forward without telling him what to do. That result is what we want to see, empowered children maintaining responsibility and moving forward.

When the Coach Has Authority

Given the non-directive nature of coaching, it can be challenging to apply these mindsets and skills when we hold a position of authority, such as a supervisor or parent.

A large part of the problem in using coaching skills in an authority role is our misconception that authority necessitates or gives us the right to be directive. Despite all our talk of being empowering servant leaders, our society still defaults to command and control when it comes to leadership. Hand someone a title with a bit of authority and they will often shift their leadership style to a command-and-control approach. The old saying, "power corrupts," seems to be mirrored in our everyday attempts to coach in situations where we feel we have authority. It doesn't have to be this way.

To truly grow an organization, we must reach organizational objectives *and* develop the capacity of the people in our organization. Supervisors who micro-manage employees may achieve the first goal, but not the second. An effective supervisor seeks to accomplish the two goals simultaneously, reaching organizational objectives while developing employees. The same goes for parents. We want to see our children get good grades, while developing their character, discipline, and study habits. It's not one or the other. It's both.

In an authority relationship, freedom of self-management is negotiated and earned. It is within this area of freedom that we can have coaching conversations. A supervisor who wishes to use a coaching approach more often in her leadership style needs to keep this scope of freedom in mind.

As I think back to the supervisors I most appreciate, each one set clear expectations and used a coaching approach with me. Their expectations narrowed the field so that I understood what areas of the project were open for my ideas, changes, and innovations, or when I just needed to follow their directions.

When coaching those you have authority over, it's important to clarify how much freedom the employee has to decide, plan, and act on his or her own. A coaching approach usually takes place within these areas of freedom. Having and agreeing on clear expectations is the first step.

As the person is able and willing, expand the areas of freedom to allow the employee greater input. Draw out his or her creativity and ownership of their work.

To further illustrate how this dynamic works, let's divide a project into four generic parts:

1. Objectives—the project's purpose, goals, and outcomes.
2. Strategies—the larger plans to reach objectives.
3. Methods—the specific ways that strategies will be carried out.
4. Tasks—the day-to-day working.

Which of these four parts are open for the employee to decide and act on?

For example, imagine a mission organization that is seeking funding for their staff members. The objective is that every staff member is fully funded. The strategy is that each staff member is responsible to raise their financial support through their own network of friends and churches. The methods and the tasks might be left up to the individuals to decide. In this case, a series of coaching conversations might center on the methods and day-to-day tasks the staff member will use to raise their ongoing financial support.

What if the staff member questions the strategy? Perhaps this person would like to start a business as part of their funding strategy. Is that acceptable? If the supervisor and organization are open to discussing this strategy, then this could be a coaching topic. If not, then that fact should be clearly communicated to the staff member, so as to not build false hope. Coaching would then be limited to how to achieve the approved strategy, that is, raising financial support.

The same holds true in a parenting situation. That a 15-year-old will go to school is not up for discussion, however, how the teenager gets there—bus, walking, a ride with a friend, etc.—might be. Clarify the boundaries and then coach within those boundaries. Outside the boundaries, you may need to be more directive.

One other difference in coaching those you have authority over is that the coaching topics will be more limited. If you are in a work relationship, coaching conversations will naturally focus on work topics. Don't expect an employee to open up about their marriage, children, and lifelong dreams. Because of your authority relationship with them, he or she may not feel comfortable discussing these things with you. Other people in their life might be more appropriate to coach on these topics.

Mentors With Coaching Skills

A Mentor is someone who has experience in a particular area and shares that learning with a protégé. Mentors provide knowledge, advice, guidance, correction and encouragement in their field of expertise. A mentor usually works within their profession, because they are offering their experience and advice.

People look for mentoring to learn something, but not necessarily to be taught. I'm reminded of Winston Churchill's reflection, "I am always ready to learn although I do not always like being taught."

A mentor usually works within their profession,
because they are offering their experience and advice.

Integrating coaching skills will make your mentoring relationships tremendously more effective. I like the way Novo President, Sam Metcalf, once described it, "My best mentors were excellent coaches." That's it, exactly! Great mentors know how to use non-directive coaching practices—listening and asking questions—to draw out from their protégé first before advising.

Adult learning theory tells us that adults want to be in control of their own learning. They may desire help but want to decide what they will learn and then take a practical, problem-oriented path to solutions.

The Mentor who applies coaching skills such as active listening and powerful questioning, will discover the protégé's needs and then be able to share more specifically and briefly regarding those needs.

Just as important, using coaching skills will help the protégé create their own plan of action, a plan that flows out of who they are, not who the Mentor is. As discussed earlier, when people create their own action steps they take greater responsibility in completing them.

Protégé: I'm thinking about going back to school to get a master's degree. You know me and my situation, what do you think?

Mentor: What brings this up?

Protégé: I've been in my position the longest. But it seems like everyone around me is being promoted. I thought a master's degree might get me promoted.

Mentor: A master's degree might help, but there are other more immediate ways you could increase your value to your company. Would you be interested in discussing those?

Protégé: Sure.

Mentor: One thing I'd suggest is to make sure you're completing your job assignments on time and on your own. I've noticed you hesitate to move forward without first consulting your supervisor. It is important to keep her informed at crucial junctures, but you ask her to make decisions that are really your responsibility to make.

Protégé: I don't want to mess up anything.

Mentor: What's behind that feeling?

Protégé: I really need this job. If my supervisor makes decisions on my work, I know she'll be happy with the results. Stepping out more on my own feels risky.

Mentor: There's some validity in your thinking. However, it's also just as likely that your supervisor isn't seeing you take full responsibility for your current work, so why promote you?

Protégé: I hadn't thought of it that way before.

Mentor: Assume that your level of work is 80%. What would you do differently to see it go to 90%? 95%?

(The discussion continues by looking for practical actions the Protégé can take to improve his or her work.)

Notice how in this dialogue the Mentor shares advice, yet, with most exchanges the Mentor either leads with a question to draw out the protégé or probes more deeply after making a statement. Giving advice is easy. Getting people to make practical use of it is best helped by coaching the person through their plans for implementation. The Mentor can remove barriers along the way.

Instructors Who Help People Learn

Instructors, Pastors, and Teachers often believe their role is to teach. No, it's to help students to learn. There's a big difference between these two concepts. If we're there to teach, then we will determine what the student needs to know, pass on our wisdom (usually by talking to them), and then tell them how to apply it.

Instructors often believe their role is to teach. No, it's to help students to learn. There's a big difference!

If you integrate coaching mindsets into instruction, you'll approach the student from a different perspective and achieve different results. For example, coaches know that the main reason people don't apply learning isn't that they don't have enough information, it's something else. Just this principle, applied to a workshop or lecture or Sunday School class, changes everything. In my case, after learning to coach, I cut the information in my teaching by half and doubled the time focused on practicing and applying what we were learning. The result was participants put the inspiration and information I communicated into practice.

When designing workshops, speaking engagements, and classes, I divide the available learning time into three big blocks:

1. **Information and inspiration from me on the topic.** I give enough that the learner engages with the topic and is willing to try it out.

2. **Reflection and discussion.** Using questions, I give the learners time to think about the topic and relate it to their own experience. Often this is done through small group discussion or an exercise where they write something on posters. Physical movement helps the learning process.

3. **Practice and application.** Most learning events I have attended didn't include practice. And application was limited to a question the audience was to reflect on as they left. This is a mistake. Practicing the learning topic generates more learning, questions, and motivation for further learning. Debriefing the practice to draw out learning and difficulties reinforces the experience.

Some of the best learning happens in the moments after a small group discussion or practice during the debrief. Done well, the instructor coaches the person who comments or asks a question, with the rest of the group listening in and learning.

Consider a discipleship relationship. Usually, discipleship meetings look a lot like teaching one-on-one or in small groups. Teaching is a very appropriate part of the disciple-making process. However, I still maintain my three-part outline of teaching, discussion, and practice. Coaching skills can particularly enhance application in discipleship.

After studying a Bible passage, the Disciple-Maker can ask, "What will you do, based on your understanding of this passage?" Coaching a person to make specific, concrete, application is the essence of obedience (Matthew 28:20).

Information rarely changes people's behavior, but experience often does. My biggest objective in coaching, as well as teaching, is to help people make mental shifts so they are willing to get into action.

Coaching Beyond Borders

It might surprise you to hear that coaching works well, some claim even better, by phone rather than in person. According to one study, 47% of professional coaches worldwide coach primarily over the telephone or Internet voice-to-voice services such as Skype.[25] This means that anyone in the world can get coaching help, and if you have a telephone or Skype you can coach someone regardless of where they live.

One local church pastor I know tested this assertion by coaching long distance with great success. Here's his story.

Every year, First Baptist Church sends two interns to serve with a partner ministry in India for six months. In preparation for their moving to India the interns receive extensive training. "Despite this training," says Paul Santiago, a pastor at First Baptist, "we had a hit and miss record with interns. Some did well. Others were overwhelmed with needs and unable to deal with culture shock on their own. As a missions pastor, I wanted to help, but felt limited because of geography. I am 6,000 miles away. I called occasionally to encourage them. But it didn't seem to make much difference."

"Things changed after I learned to coach," Pastor Paul continued. He began to have coaching conversations weekly with the interns, using the free computer-to-computer Skype service. "This past year I've had coaching conversations regularly with the interns. I found that small issues never grew into larger problems. Overall, the interns' experiences were much more fruitful. I was fully engaged with them during their internship, even from 6,000 miles away. When they returned home, I knew many of the details of their rich experience. I've continued coaching some of the interns even after their return."

Who do you know that could use some coaching help? Forget about distance and geographical borders. Using the phone or your computer you could coach a student away at college, a relative in another city, a co-worker in another office, or someone in your town—even when you're otherwise too busy to meet.

Offer to Coach

The easiest place to use your coaching skills is in those one-on-one relationships you already have. If you are already meeting regularly in a discipleship or mentoring relationship, reframe how you work together using the coaching tools you've learned. Listen and ask more questions to help the person reflect more deeply. Hold back your own stories and advice and draw out theirs. Ask the person you are meeting with to create a couple of action steps. Make it natural.

You don't necessarily have to tell them what you are doing. Experiencing a coaching conversation is much better than hearing an explanation about one.

Experiencing a coaching conversation is much better than hearing an explanation about one.

Offer to coach people. Some people, knowing that I coach others, ask me to coach them. But most of the coaching relationships I've had were a result of me offering to coach.

If you don't offer to coach others, people may assume that you are too busy to coach them. Or perhaps they don't know what coaching is or are unaware of how helpful it might be in their situation. If you are willing, then offer!

Here's how I might offer to coach someone through a casual conversation. After hearing Jeff share a difficulty, I said, "What you are talking about sounds challenging. I wonder if you could use some additional help with it?"

"What kind of help?"

"I often meet with people for an hour every week or so for what I call 'coaching conversations.' I help them understand their situation more clearly and create action steps to move forward."

Jeff replied, "I'm not sure what to do with this problem."

"I'd be happy to help. Would you like to get together one morning this week? We could meet, and if you'd like to continue after that, we can. It's up to you."

"What does this cost?" Jeff asked.

"Buy me a cup of coffee. It's my pleasure to help out."

Offering to coach others is as easy as letting them know you are willing to have a conversation with them. Once you've successfully coached a few people, word will begin to get around and others might come to you. But don't wait for someone to ask you, take the initiative and offer to get together and talk.

Next Steps

*"Whatever you have learned or received or heard
from me, or seen in me—put it into practice.
And the God of peace will be with you."*
—Philippians 4:9

Now that you have a coaching model and a number of skills, how can you *grow* from here?

Coaching as a skill set has moved from its infancy to become a well-developed helping process with mindsets, skills, expectations, and outcomes. Those wishing to grow in their coaching ability now have many resources available to them. Here are a few.

Learning From Books

When I became serious about learning to coach, I turned to books. For three years, I read books and practiced what I learned. I focused on becoming a better listener, and then began to ask open rather than yes-no questions. I used a simple model for conversations that helped me focus longer on reflection and discovery before moving on to action steps. Eventually, I developed The COACH Model® and now use that.

My progress was slow, but I saw fruit from my efforts. The young Indonesians I worked with at the time gained greater awareness regarding their character and ministry focus. I was amazed as they put these insights into action using ideas that had never occurred to me.

Not everything was rosy. By habit, I was still too quick to share my ideas and advice. But as I disciplined myself to listen, ask questions, and allow my Indonesian coachees to make their own decisions, I saw their confidence and judgment skills increase. They developed as leaders. I helped them not just by telling or teaching, but by drawing them out using powerful questions and allowing the Holy Spirit to lead instead of me.

After a few years of practicing coaching in this way, my wife and I attended a professional coaching training with a marketplace organization. We learned a lot, and also confirmed what we were already practicing.

All this to say, don't discount what you can accomplish after reading a book like this. Go back and create your own action plans using the instructions in this book. Put into practice what you've read, and you will see results.

Develop Your Mindset

The ability to coach begins with the coach's mindset. How do you want to *be* as you coach? Here are some helpful mindsets to pay attention to and consider.

- Look for the Holy Spirit to teach and remind, both you and the coachee.
- Move from problem-solver to solution-discoverer.
- Shift from teacher to fellow learner.
- Value the coachee's ideas and solutions over your own.

As you engage in coaching conversations be aware of what is happening *in you*. Right after a conversation, take a few minutes to reflect on the following questions.[26] For complete instructions on how to self-reflect to grow personally and professionally, see my book, *The Reflective Journal for Coaches*.

Think about what was happening in you during the coaching conversation:

- What thoughts did you have?
- What emotions were you feeling?
- When were you distracted or not fully present in the conversation? What caused this?
- What would you do differently next time?

It is even better to have someone else coach you through these questions. It helps to meet with someone else who wants to improve their coaching skills and is willing to discuss these questions.

Additional Training

Many in ministry call themselves a "coach" or describe their ministry function as "coaching." More and more, the people we minister to are going to read and hear about coaching and will ask, "Where did you get your coaching training?" Coaching has grown into a defined skill set and taken on unique characteristics that produce effective results.

Coach training that follows professional coaching standards is a huge benefit to those in positions of leadership.

To excel in coaching, like anything in life, requires study and practice. Learning to coach well requires getting together with an experienced coach to learn and practice the art and skills of coaching. Specialized coaching training has emerged to meet this need. This training should consist of at three essential practices:[27]

1. Specific training on core coaching skills.
2. Practice coaching others and being coached.
3. Expert observation and feedback on your coaching.

There are numerous workshops that refer to coaching. Many do not use coaching in the same sense that this book uses it. Some workshops use the term "coach" quite broadly, considering it any type of one-on-one helping. Often the workshop is focused specifically on who will be coached, like students, new believers, church planters, or pastors. The training prepares participants to help these types of people. Often this help is in the form of teaching or training, rather than coaching.

To excel in coaching, like anything in life,
requires study and practice.

Other types of training focus on using a specific tool, process, or assessment. In these cases, the focus is on interpreting or processing the tool or assessment, like Strengths Finder or DiSC, for example. They call the approach "coaching," but what you learn at the workshop is how to interpret the assessment results. Once you know how to coach well, using these specialty tools or assessments can be a benefit to those you coach.

Coach-specific training is specifically focused on non-directive coaching mindsets and skills. Many organizations offer this type of training, each with their own perspective, but with similar basic coaching skills. I developed coaching training from a Christian worldview and with business and ministry settings in mind for application. Other Christian organizations prepare people to start their own Christian Life Coaching businesses, while marketplace organizations teach coaching from secular, psychological, self-help, or even New Age perspectives. It's important to understand the organization's worldview perspective and the intended setting in which you will coach others.

My organization has trained thousands of people to coach in their ministry settings. In our experience, short coaching workshops of three days or longer give potential coaches the instruction or guided practice they need to reach the effectiveness they desire as coaches.

We offer several International Coach Federation (ICF) approved certificate programs[28] for Christian leaders. Taught from a Christian perspective using the principles in this book, these programs equip Christian leaders at the highest professional coaching standards.

Unlike some marketplace settings, coaching topics of faith or ministry are welcome in our workshops. No need to hide or gloss-over the deepest aspects of life. We encourage participants to integrate on all levels: spiritual, character, family, professional, cultural, community, etc. Of course, the coaching skills we teach are completely compatible with and non-offensive to those who are not Christian.

For a detailed look at the three essential practices of effective coaching training, see Appendix 2.

Ready, Set, Go

"I can't do it." That's often the response I hear from people attending a one-day coaching training.

"I don't ask good enough questions." That's a response I hear from some people attending a three-day coaching training.

"Who would want me to coach them?" That's a response I hear from some people who attended a seven-day coaching training.

Are you catching the pattern here? It doesn't matter how much training you have received, when you are doing something new, you rarely feel ready, confident, or qualified.

Moses felt the same way. He spent 40 years tending sheep in the desert when God asked him to lead Israel out of captivity in Egypt. Read their conversation:

> "Moses said to the Lord, 'Pardon your servant, Lord. I have never been eloquent, neither in the past nor since you have spoken to your servant. I am slow of speech and tongue.' The Lord said to him, 'Who gave human beings their mouths? Who makes them deaf or mute? Who gives them sight or makes them blind? Is it not I, the Lord? Now go; I will help you speak and will teach you what to say.'" [29]

Going back to John 14:26, the Holy Spirit will teach and remind you. You must do your part in disciplining yourself to use the skills you are learning. There are many ways to get started in coaching others. All of them involve stepping outside your comfort zone and doing it. This takes faith.

Don't expect that you'll be a master coach right from the start. It takes time and a lot of hard work. You *will* be helpful to people as you coach, more helpful than you are now, and that will produce a fruitful impact in the lives of those with whom you interact.

Appendix 1
Sample Coaching Agreement

Coaching agreements help to clarify the expectations of the coaching relationship. It's important for people you coach to understand what coaching is and isn't and what are their responsibilities. Use this simple agreement as a tool to discuss the coaching relationship.

Coaching Agreement

Prior to entering into a personal coaching relationship, please carefully read the following agreement and indicate you understand and agree by signing below.

1. I understand that personal coaching is a relationship I have with a personal coach that is designed to help me develop and establish short and long-term goals and develop and implement strategies to achieve those goals that may involve all areas of my life.
2. I understand that I am fully responsible for my choices and decisions and may discontinue coaching at any time.
3. I understand that we will coach by phone, and I will make every effort to be ready for the call on time.

4. I understand that coaching conversations are confidential, and my coach will not share our discussion with others without my permission.
5. I understand that for coach credentialing purposes my name and contact information, but not the contents of my coaching, may be given to the International Coach Federation and other qualified organizations.

Coachee Signature: _____ Date: _____

Appendix 2
Three Essential Practices of Effective Coaching Training

Professional coaching associations have researched best practices and set standards for effective coaching. The largest of these associations is the International Coach Federation (ICF) with 34,000 members around the world. The ICF identified 11 core coaching competencies and a list of sub-points under each that coaches must master to be able to coach well.

From the ICF's standards we can determine three essential practices of effective coaching training:

1. Live Coaching Instruction

Becoming an effective coach requires specialized "live" coaching training. Whatever you do, it needs to be live, interactive, and in the moment.

You can't learn to coach from watching a video, reading a book, listening to a webinar, working through an online course, or sitting in an auditorium with hundreds of other people. Written or recorded material can serve to supplement live training, but it will never replace it. This is why the ICF won't approve training that isn't "voice-to-voice," meaning the instructor and participant are able to interact.

Beyond live instruction, there are a few characteristics of the instructor that are important to your successful learning. Many people may be able to coach well, but training others to coach well is another thing entirely.

The coaching instructor should model masterful coaching.

I shouldn't need to write this, but it's surprising how many people teach what they can't actually do well themselves. Look for instructors who hold an ICF coach credential. An ICF coach credential requires the person to have taken coach-specific training and passed an exam process based on coaching skills.

The coaching instructor should be able to teach coaching mindsets and skills.

I've participated in a number of coaching workshops where the instructor was unable to teach how to ask powerful questions, "because question asking is intuitive and you have to feel it in the moment." Rubbish. This response is an indicator the instructor hasn't reflected deeply enough to understand how to pass question-asking skills onto others. "If you can't explain it simply," Einstein is attributed to saying, "you don't understand it well enough."

The coaching instructor should incorporate discovery and practice.

Coaching training should be interactive and discovery-focused with large blocks of the time invested not in passing on information but in practicing skills. Surprisingly, some excellent coaches turn into rambling lecturers when standing in front of a group. Just like in coaching, in training, instructors must focus on the participant's learning. Instructors need to manage their egos, information, and advice.

The coaching instructor's worldview matters.

We all make sense of life by interpreting it according to our worldview. Mine is based on my Christian faith, my experience living in different cultures for 20 years in Asia, and my work background. If you take a course from an instructor with a counseling background, you'll get more of a counseling perspective. Business background, yep, a larger number of business examples. A Buddhist will relate coaching and human dynamics to their understanding of the world. Diversity is fine to a point but try to match the instructor's worldview and background to your own.

2. Live Coaching Practice

In my coaching training I work for a time balance of one third information from the instructor, one third interaction among the participants discussing and reflecting, and one third practicing the skills. The last third is the most difficult to design and incorporate into a workshop, but it results in the greatest impact on learning.

Effective coaching training will incorporate these 3 types of practice:

Practice individual coaching skills.

By isolating and creating ways to practice each coaching skill or mindset, participants can get specific and drill down to become proficient in each. Practice every skill individually—asking powerful questions, generating feedback, forming action steps, etc. The better each skill can be defined and isolated, the easier it will be to learn.

Practice coaching with other participants.

Combine the individual skills and practice by engaging in coaching conversations with other participants. This type of practice is like riding a bicycle with training wheels. Since the other participants know what the coach is trying to do, conversations flow more easily. It's a good way to pull the skills together and use them in coaching conversations to gain confidence. A bonus is having the chance to experience *being* coached.

Practice coaching with other people.

"Real world" coaching practice is challenging. Find people who are ready and willing to be coached. Then, coach them using the skills and mindsets you've learned, without falling back into your old ways. Each person you coach will be a different experience for you. Some are more reflective. Some are more action oriented. Some bring topics that match your interests. Some move forward quickly. Some seem to make no progress. It takes a variety of coachees and dozens of coaching conversations to be able to consistently coach well. In fact, the ICF considers 100 coaching hours with at least 8 people the minimum experience for their first level of coach certification.

Nothing can replace actually practicing coaching skills and mindsets. Effective coaching courses will facilitate a lot of practice—especially during the course itself.

Effective coaching courses will facilitate a lot
of practice, especially during the course itself.

---

3. Live Coaching Feedback

The more you practice the better you get, right? Not necessarily.

Blues guitarist Howard Roberts is referred to as "The Jazz Master" due to his unsurpassed skill. His secret was to never practice a mistake. The more you practice in the correct way, the better you'll become. But if you practice a mistake, you'll ingrain that mistake into your behavior.

Practicing 100 hours of coaching is worse than not practicing at all if you're practicing mistakes. The trouble is, without observed feedback from an experienced instructor, you won't know what you're doing that is a mistake or what you're not doing that you should be doing.

We incorporate written observation and feedback into our training. Our instructors observe participants coaching and then give specific feedback, highlighting strengths and suggesting points of improvement. This is essential and another reason why non-interactive learning methods—books, videos, webinars, etc.—are not effective.

The ICF requires what it calls "mentor coaching" to be incorporated into approved coaching training programs. This is 10 hours of observed coaching feedback specifically around improving your coaching skills. It works.

Practice is essential, but more than practice, you have to practice the correct things. Without observed feedback, you'll repeat mistakes and reinforce wrong ways of doing it.

Look for coaching training that includes live instruction, live practice, and live feedback.

Which Coaching Training Courses Should I Take?

Some coaching courses have been approved by the ICF. Just as individual coaches are examined for certification, so are coaching courses that training schools offer.

A study in 2015[30] revealed 89% of professional coaches received training that was accredited or approved by a professional coaching organization. One short-cut to shifting through various coaching training options is to check to see if it is an ICF-approved training program. A course approved by the ICF will be screened by them to meet the training standards described above.

My own coaching training programs have all been approved by the ICF and illustrates why approval indicates quality. The approval process was long, detailed, and rigorous. We had to make a number of improvements to our already successful programs in order for the ICF to approve them. I submitted our courses to the ICF examination process, and the subsequent renewal processes, to make sure we offer training that meets the marketplace's highest standards.

Our Coaching Mastery Certificate Program[31] is an ICF-approved training program that provides everything you need to become an ICF Associate Certified Coach. It has 73 hours of live instruction, 10 hours of live feedback (mentor coaching), and plenty of practice to enable you to get the 100 client coaching hours you need.

By taking an ICF-approved coaching program you can apply for an ICF coach credential using an easier and less expensive application process.

Appendix 3
How to Become an ICF Certified Coach

Coaches with specialized training and a top-level coaching certification will be more effective coaches and will more easily attract clients. The gold-standard in coach certifications are from the International Coach Federation (ICF). While famous coaches and schools can and do create their own coach certifications, the ICF, as the world's largest coaching association, sets the bar high. I'll share my insider knowledge of how you can become an ICF certified coach.

Coach certifications are confusing to many people. After 8 years on two ICF chapter board of directors, including a period as President of the ICF Washington State Chapter, I've fielded a lot of questions about coach training programs and certifications.

Part of the problem is, as the number of coaches has grown, many organizations have popped up offering coach credentials, licenses, and certifications. It's great business to get coaches to pay you $179 a year to be "certified." Then there are the famous leadership gurus who offer their own coach certification for $4,000 that consists of watching videos and attending a conference.

Organizations use many different terms to differentiate themselves, but also to make themselves sound more attractive to potential students.

The terms sound similar, but differences are in the details—and are important.

The first step toward sorting out the coach credentialing process is understanding what all the different terms mean.

Certificate: A document given by training schools that recognize a student has completed a coaching course. Any school can issue certificates. Find out which, if any, coaching association has approved the school's courses. Also, note the length of training varies by the course. You can get a certificate for a 12-hour or a 75-hour course, for example. Obviously, the learning will be different between them.

Certified: Indicates that a person has been examined and achieved a standard. The key to understanding this is: what standard? And who is behind that standard? A certification is only as good as the rigors of standards behind the organization that grants it. Professional associations provide an external and objective validation of training programs and coaches. I've written elsewhere why you should get your coaching credential from an association and not your coach training school.[32]

Credential: Often synonymous with Certified. A certified coach receives a coach credential.

Licensed: Indicates someone is approved by an organization to use their methodology or material.

Diploma: Echoes back to higher education. Ask what college or government association approved the granting of this diploma. If there isn't any approval, then the diploma is the same as a non-approved certificate.

I recommend getting a coaching certificate from an ICF-approved training program and then applying to the ICF for a coach credential. I'll explain why.

Why the ICF?

A coach credential is only as good as the rigors of standards behind the organization that grants it. As the world's largest professional coaching association, the ICF provides an external and objective validation of training programs and coaches.

The ICF is:

Established, in 1995 with 34,000 members in 145 countries as of 2018.

Diverse, with more members outside the United States than in it.

Professional, setting and maintaining high industry coaching standards.

Unbiased, without ties to one particular school or methodology.

Supportive, with chapters and learning opportunities around the world.

Tough, you must demonstrate excellent coaching to be certified.

You can find easier and cheaper ways to be "certified" as a coach, but they will not push you to coaching excellence like the ICF will. No one is looking for a coach who cuts corners, but a coach who is effective. The ICF provides objective validation of a coach's effectiveness.

A coach credential is only as good as the rigors
of standards behind the organization that grants it.

The 3 Levels of ICF Coach Certification

The ICF offers coaches three levels of coach certifications based on coaching competency. Each level has an increasingly higher standard.

The ICF separates their coaching credentials by the 3 essential practices of effective coaching training. They are: live instruction, live practice, and live feedback. The ICF's requirements for each level of coach certification follows these three practices.

A minimum number of hours of coaching training and experience has been identified that will most likely mean the coach has reached that level's standard of coaching competency. In addition to these minimum requirements, coaches must demonstrate their coaching competency through an increasingly rigorous examination process.

Associate Certified Coach

- 60+ hours of coaching instruction.
- 100+ hours of practice with coaching clients.
- 10 hours feedback (mentor coaching) with a qualified coach.

Professional Certified Coach

- 125+ hours of coaching instruction.
- 500+ hours of practice with coaching clients.
- 10 hours feedback (mentor coaching) with a qualified coach.

Master Certified Coach

- 200+ hours of coaching instruction.
- 2500+ hours of practice with coaching clients.
- 10 hours feedback (mentor coaching) with a qualified coach.

Some people new to coaching view these requirements as hoops to jump through to get a credential. As a coaching instructor, I see the profound differences in the coaching mindsets and coaching skills at each credential level. With each coach credential level comes increasing coaching effectiveness. For a coach to achieve each skill level, it takes more and more focus along with specialized training, practice, and feedback.

Few untrained coaches can pass the ICF's certification process, regardless of how many people they've coached. A coach credential by the ICF verifies the coach has reached a level of effectiveness in their coaching. You don't need a piece of paper, but you do need the skills to make a real difference in the lives of the people you coach.

Getting an ICF coach credential isn't easy. But neither is coaching effectively. By doing the work to reach the high standards of an ICF credential you'll become a more effective coach, able to deliver better results to coachees. And that's worth working for.

I invite you to take a look at our coaching training programs at http://CreativeResultsManagement.com.

Acknowledgements

"It is very easy to overestimate the importance of our own achievements in comparison with what we owe others."
—Dietrich Bonhoeffer

This book is about learning. More specifically, it's about learning with the help of a coach. Coaches empower people to think more deeply, tap into the broad resources that surround them, and make their own informed decisions. It's *the* critical leadership skill set that supercharges interaction with other people.

Many people assisted me in learning the lessons communicated in this book. Steve Ogne first introduced me to coaching in 1994 and remained my friend and coaching guru, until his passing in 2015. J. Robert Clinton, Gary Mayes, and Terry Walling influenced my paradigm of leadership development. I learned to coach in Indonesia, inflicting Herman, Jimmy, Medi, Mery, Michael, and Rosgentina with my early attempts.

Takeshi Takazawa and I saw the multicultural relevance of coaching[33] as we taught three-day workshops using early versions of these materials for locals in Cambodia, China, England, Hungary, Indonesia, Japan, Lebanon, Russia, and Singapore. Many innovations were made along the way.

In October 2006, Lori Webb and I led our first professional-length coaching training program for Christian leaders. In the years since then, we have trained many thousands of leaders as coaches. Dave DeVries, Charles Hooper, Félix Ortiz, Katie Reid, Kevin Stebbings, Lori Webb, Bryan Wintersteen, and Kim Zovak of the Creative Results Management training team have assisted me in making improvements along the way.

A wholehearted "thank you!" goes out to each person who contributed to my thinking and practice.

I am grateful to Dr. Gary R. Collins for contributing the Foreword. Lisa Meaney edited the original text, creating a book that reads much more easily. Pam McCrum edited the revised edition. Any mistakes are mine. I appreciate the kind folks at Morgan James Publishing for getting this book out to a much wider audience.

Lori, it's been quite a journey. You've been there every step of the way. I'm so glad to go with you.

Finally, I wish to express my deep gratitude to the many thousands of Christian leaders who have read this book, taken one of our courses, and most of all, coached others as a result. Their focus on improving their coaching skills has resulted in countless changed lives.

Most examples in this book are based on actual coaching conversations. Names, locations, and details are changed and are composites of different coaching conversations for purposes of confidentiality. Any resemblance to real persons, living or dead, is purely coincidental.

Endnotes

1   I am not alone in this. As people learn about new things, they can often talk about them far earlier than they can do them. Peter Senge, *The Fifth Discipline: The Art and Practice of The Learning Organization* (NY: Currency Doubleday, 1990), 377.

2   Julia Milner, & Trenton Milner (2018). "Managers think they're good at coaching. They're not." *Harvard Business Review.* Retrieved from https://hbr. org/2018/08/managers-think-theyre-good-at-coaching-theyre-not

3   This is an advantage for Christians. However, it's not necessary to explicitly refer to God in order to reflect on calling. Everyday language can achieve similar ends. "What do you understand your calling in life to be?" "What potential in you is waiting to be released?" Of course, answers are incomplete without God's perspective.

4   Richard Foster, *Celebration of Disciplines: The Path to Spiritual Growth* (New York: HarperCollins, 1988), 185.

5   Keith R. Anderson and Randy D. Reese, *Spiritual Mentoring: A Guide for Seeking and Giving Direction* (Downers Grove, IL: Intervarsity Press, 1999), 21.

6   Chris Argyris and Donald Schon, *Organizational Learning: A Theory of Action Perspective* (Reading MA: Addison-Wesley, 1978).

7   Steven R. Covey, *The 7 Habits of Highly Effective People: Powerful Lessons in Personal Change* (New York: Fireside, 1989).

8   Malcom Knowles, et al., *Andragogy in Action: Applying Modern Principles of Adult Education* (San Francisco: Jossey-Bass, 1984), Appendix D.

9   Google the words "snow on car commercial" to find it.

10 Lyle E. Schaller, *The interventionist: A conceptual framework and questions for parish consultants, intentional interim ministers, church champions, pastors considering a new call, denominational executives, the recently arrived*

pastor, counselors, and other intentional interventionists in congregational life (Nashville, TN: Abingdon Press, 1997), 15.

11   Ibid., 15.

12   Jane Vella, *Learning to Listen Learning to Teach: The Power of Dialogue in Educating Adults* (San Francisco: Jossey Bass, 1994), 73.

13   Peter Block, *The Answer to How is Yes: Acting on What Matters* (San Francisco: Berrett-Koehler, 2002), Preface.

14   I've actually never asked WWJD. I added this question to the list make my youth pastor friends smile.

15   John Whitmore, *Coaching For Performance: Growing People, Performance and Purpose* (3th ed.) (London: Nicholas Berkley, 2002), 139.

16   "Right Answer" thinking and other blocks to creativity are explored by Roger von Oech, *A Whack on the Side of the Head: How to Unlock Your Mind for Innovation* (NY: Warner Books, 1983).

17   John Kotter, *Leading Change* (Boston, MA: Harvard Business School Press, 1996).

18   Half of this book was written in Singapore, the other half near Seattle.

19   George T. Doran, "There's a S.M.A.R.T. Way to Write Management's Goals and Objectives," *Management Review* 70 (November 1981), Issue 11(AMA FORUM): 35-36.

20   This was a previous action step. Listing all the different activities and relationships a person has and ranking them according to how stressful they are right now. The exercise increases awareness, giving the coachee information to act on.

21   Jeffrey Schwartz, a research psychiatrist at UCLA School of Medicine, has done fascinating and conclusive research on self-directed neuroplasticity of the brain. A recent, practical book is: Jeffrey M. Schwartz and Rebecca Gladding, *You Are Not Your Brain: The Four Step Solution for Changing Bad Habits, Ending Unhealthy Thinking, and Taking Control of Your Life* (NY: Avery, 2010).

22   For an engaging summary of studies see Richard E. Nisbett, *The Geography of Thought: How Asians and Westerners Think Differently…and Why?* (New York: Free Press, 2003), 53-56, or Aik Kwang Ng, *Why Asians are Less Creative Than Westerners* (Singapore: Prentice Hall, 2001).

23   Terry Borton, *Reach, Touch, and Teach: Student Concerns and Process Education* (New York: McGraw-Hill, 1970).

24   Thomas L. Friedman, *The Lexus and the Olive Tree: Understanding Globalization* (NY: Anchor Books, 2000), 370.

25   *ICF Global Client Coaching Study: Executive Summary* (Lexington, Kentucky: International Coach Federation, April 2009).

26   Keith E. Webb, *The Reflective Journal for Coaches* (Bellevue, WA: Active Results LLC, 2015.)

27 See Appendix 2: Three Essential Practices of Effective Coaching Training.

28 You can find more information about our certificate programs at: http://creativeresultsmanagement.com

29 Exodus 4:10-11.

30 *2016 ICF Global Coaching Study: Executive Summary* (Lexington, Kentucky: International Coach Federation, 2016).

31 See http://creativeresultsmanagement.com/mastery

32 See, Keith E. Webb, "Want To Be A "Certified Coach"?" at https://keithwebb.com/want-to-be-a-certified-coach/

33 For more, see Keith E. Webb, "Cross-Cultural Coaching," in Denise Wright, et al, *Coaching in Asia: The First Decade* (Singapore: Candid Creation Publishing, 2010).

About the Author

Keith E. Webb, DMin, is an ICF Professional Certified Coach, author, and speaker specializing in leadership development. He is the founder and President of Creative Results Management, a global training organization focused on equipping ministry leaders.

For 20 years, Keith lived in Japan, Indonesia, and Singapore. These experiences led him to question conventional leadership practices. Now he writes and speaks on topics related to leadership.

Keith created the COACH Model® and a series of International Coach Federation (ICF) approved coaching training programs. Using his humorous and practical style of delivery, he has delivered leadership development programs to Christian leaders around the world.

He is the author of *The COACH Model of Christian Leaders, Coaching In Ministry, The Reflective Journal for Coaches, Overcoming Spiritual Barriers in Japan,* and is co-author of *Coaching In Asia.* Keith posts leadership articles at keithwebb.com.

Keith lives near Seattle with Lori, his wife.

COACH Model® Resources

The COACH Model® Card

The COACH Model® Card is an easy-to-use five step guide to a coaching conversation.

The COACH Model® Bookmark

A bookmark with The COACH Model® and questions from 18 different angles to help raise awareness.

Coaching In Ministry

Learn practical ways to develop the people around you and multiply your ministry impact through coaching.

Coaching allows you to facilitate the development of both skills and character in other people, while getting ministry done.

Order from **store.keithwebb.com**

Printed in the USA
CPSIA information can be obtained
at www.ICGtesting.com
JSHW022335140824
68134JS00019B/1489